Praise for
The Buddha's Guide to Gratitude

"Practicing gratitude is like taking your vitamins—you don't just take them when you're sick; you also have to take them to stay healthy."

—**Louise Harmon, author of** *Happiness A–Z*

"The most magnetic trait of all time is gratitude! If you want to transform your outlook and your life, read and enjoy The Buddha's Guide to Gratitude.*"*

—**Susan Seton, author of** *Simple Pleasures of the Home*

"Gratitude is a choice. When we choose to focus on what is right in our lives instead of what is missing, our appreciation for life can give us each a sense of purpose. This book is a guide to increasing your happiness quotient."

—Nina Lesowitz, author of *Living Life as a Thank You*

"Becca Anderson has lit the path of gratitude, and spurred us to make this important spiritual practice the center of our lives. The meditations, exercises, and inspirational passages reveal the Buddhist connection to a deep understanding of the bounties of spirituality that we can put into our relationships, activities, and rituals."

—Elise Marie Collins, author of *Super Ager* and *Chakra Tonics*

The Buddha's Guide to Gratitude

THE
BUDDHA'S
GUIDE TO
GRATITUDE

The Life-Changing Power of Everyday Mindfulness

Becca Anderson

CORAL GABLES

Copyright © 2019 Becca Anderson

Published by Mango Publishing Group, a division of Mango Media Inc.

Mango is an active supporter of authors' rights to free speech and artistic expression in their books. The purpose of copyright is to encourage authors to produce exceptional works that enrich our culture and our open society.

Uploading or distributing photos, scans, or any content from this book without prior permission is theft of the author's intellectual property. Please honor the author's work as you would your own. Thank you in advance for respecting our author's rights.

For permission requests, please contact the publisher at:

Mango Publishing Group
2850 Douglas Road, 2nd Floor
Coral Gables, FL 33134 USA
info@mango.bz

The Buddha's Guide to Gratitude: The Life-Changing Power of Everyday Mindfulness
LCCN: 2019905276
BISAC: OCC010000—BODY, MIND & SPIRIT / Mindfulness & Meditation

"I don't personally believe in an arrived stated of enlightenment. I feel that being human is a constant practice of return. We have moments of clarity, and then we're confused. We have incredibly sensitive periods of being awake, and then we're numb. Being human is a very universal and a very personal practice of learning how to return when we can't get access to what we know."

—Mark Nepo

TABLE OF CONTENTS

THE PRACTICE OF CONTENTMENT

"Every day, think as you wake up: Today I am fortunate to have woken up. I am alive. I have a precious human life. I am not going to waste it. I am going to use all my energies to develop myself, to expand my heart out to others, to achieve enlightenment for the benefit of all beings. I am going to have kind thoughts toward others, I am not going to get angry, or think badly about others. I am going to benefit others as much as I can."

—His Holiness the 14th Dalai Lama

We don't need more money; we don't need greater success or fame. Right now, at this very moment, we have a mind, which is all the basic equipment we need to achieve complete happiness. When you are discontent, you always want more, more, more. Your desire can never be satisfied. But when you practice contentment, you can say to yourself, "Oh yes—I already have everything that I really need." This book contains many good ideas for practicing contentment. Do this simple thing every day; wake up, be grateful, be kind, and help others. If you do this, your life will be filled with joy.

THE BUDDHA IN YOU

"Enough is a feast."

—Buddha

According to Buddha, *"You have no cause for anything but gratitude and joy."* Being thankful is one of the most powerful tools we humans have to attain peace of mind and a measure of happiness. As it turns out, Buddha had quite a lot to say on the subject of gratitude, including citing it as one of the four keys to the Gate of Heaven. Why is this? Perhaps because of its sheer simplicity, gratefulness is available to all of us at any time. Even in the midst of over busyness, stress, and chaos, we can find plenty to be glad about. Take time to stop each day and count your blessings. This can be a prayer or a mindfulness mediation, whatever works for you. This lovely, uncomplicated approach may well change your life.

Studies show—and experts counsel—that gratitude is a key component of our own happiness. People who are grateful about events and experiences from the past, who celebrate the triumphs instead of focusing on the losses or disappointments, tend to be more satisfied in the present. In a lecture, Buddhist leader Thích Nhất Hạnh stated, "With all I have experienced in my own life, the power of gratitude stands above everything else. In your mindfulness practice, use gratitude until it becomes your way of life."

Gratitude moves us to do all kinds of things inspired by joy. Gratitude can help us transform our fears into courage, our anger into forgiveness, our isolation into belonging, and another's pain into healing. Saying "Thank you" every day will create feelings of love, compassion, and hope.

But the fact is, the art of living—for that is what we speak about when we speak of gratitude—isn't something that comes naturally to most people. Most of us need to work intentionally to increase the intensity, duration, and frequency of positive, grateful feelings—a daunting challenge indeed. But fear not, this book is here to help! I have provided you with mindful meditations, hands-on exercises, profound practices, inspiring quotations, thought-provoking questions, space for writing your own comments, and even positive "power tools" that will help you build a more grateful life. To master the art of being a gratitude practitioner, you have to take time for gratitude every day; that works for me and it will work for you. You'll be glad and oh-so-thankful you did.

As a meditation instructor, I look for many ways to introduce the skills and states of mindfulness. Sitting in silence, breathing, doing active or restorative yoga poses, or taking a walk are all ways to practice being mindful. One only needs to show up and be deeply engaged. The quotes in this book will help you live mindfully. Like a little coach you can put in your pocket, these mindful quotes guide and instruct the reader to peace and presence. I often use quotes in my yoga classes that introduce the art of mindfulness. Use them daily to give yourself a nibble of quiet and focus. Practice, practice, practice paying attention. Take these quotes and turn to them for contemplation and a deepening of your daily awakening. Use them to help you navigate the sometimes placid, occasionally murky, and periodically turbulent waters of life.

CHAPTER 1

THE PRACTICE OF GRATITUDE

"When you realize nothing is lacking, the whole world belongs to you."

—Lao Tzu

Gratitude is one of the loveliest paths to personal growth. It can be subtle. After you start approaching your life with thankfulness, you may discover that you are functioning with a "half-full mindset." For instance, maybe instead of worrying on Sunday nights about work and meetings and goals, you relax and are grateful to have work that you really enjoy. Next thing you know, your coworkers will notice that you are less stressed-out and more fun to be around, and your desk will become an oasis of positivity in the office. Your family will respond in kind, and your home will be a calmer, happier place filled with calmer, happier people. Your friends who used to call you and complain about life, now call and tell you about all the good things that are happening to them. It took a while, but eventually your aura of gratefulness took hold and bloomed.

You, my friend, have an attitude of gratitude and are making the world a better place.

Well done, reader, and please allow me to be the first to say, thank you. And I guarantee that I won't be the last. I am a big one for setting intentions, and I do so myself every morning. I intend for you to grow and soar in your wisdom. If some of the ideas, quotes, and suggestions from the "gratitude gurus" included in this book inspire you, all the better.

Are you tired of walking around with a hole in your heart? Do you need more inspiration? Gratitude has been proven to be a key component of our own happiness. Those who think abundantly will find abundance everywhere they look. In her popular book, *The Secret*, Rhonda Byrne writes, "With all that I have read and all that I have experienced in my own life using *The Secret*, the power of gratitude stands above everything else. If you do only one thing with the knowledge of this book, use gratitude until it becomes your way of life."

The recent buzz surrounding the power of gratitude is overwhelmingly positive. Jeffery Zaslow, a columnist for the *Wall Street Journal*, recently wrote that there may be a positive by-product of the troubled economic times that followed The Great Recession: a decrease in the urge to complain. "People who still have jobs are finding reasons to be appreciative. It feels unseemly to complain about not getting a raise when your neighbor is unemployed," he wrote. "Homeowners are unhappy that home values have fallen, but it's a relief to have avoided foreclosure."

Indeed, gratitude is still popping up everywhere. Turn on the TV. I recently listened as a career coach on *The Today Show* advised job seekers to put the words, "Thank you," in their job search tool kits, declaring that the key to distinguishing oneself from the masses is to send a thank-you note. Gratitude moves us to do all kinds of things, inspired by joy. Gratitude can help us transform our fears into courage, our anger into forgiveness, our isolation into belonging, and another's pain into healing. Saying "Thank you" every day will create feelings of love, compassion, and hope.

Let That Word Be Thanks

Better
than if there were thousands
of meaningless words is
one
meaningful
word
that on hearing
brings peace.
Better
than if there were thousands
of meaningless verses is
one
meaningful
verse
that on hearing
brings peace.
And better than chanting hundreds
of meaningless verses is
one
Dhamma-saying
that on hearing
brings peace.

—Dhammapada, VIII, Attributed to Buddha

Learn as You Go: How Should I Breathe When I Meditate?

Meditation often begins with a deep intake of breath and a long exhalation. But you don't have to keep breathing that way after you've started! The deep breath at the beginning is intended to refocus yourself on the moment, on what you're doing now—namely, the meditation practice. Once you're refocused, you should breathe normally, allowing your body to take care of itself again while you meditate.

"If you want to conquer the anxiety of life, live in the moment, live in the breath."

—Amit Ray

"Do not encumber your mind with useless thoughts. What good does it do to brood on the past or anticipate the future? Remain in the simplicity of the present moment."

—Dilgo Khyentse Rinpoche

"If you aren't in the moment, you are either looking forward to uncertainty, or back to pain and regret."

—Jim Carrey

". . . . ."

"The only thing that is ultimately real about your journey is the step that you are taking at this moment. That's all there ever is."

—Eckhart Tolle

"Few of us ever live in the present. We are forever anticipating what is to come or remembering what has gone."

—Louis L'Amour

"The present moment is the only time over which we have dominion."

—Thích Nhất Hạnh

"You have to remember one life, one death—this one! To enter fully the day, the hour, the moment, whether it appears as life or death, whether we catch it on the inbreath or outbreath, requires only a moment, this moment. And along with it, all the mindfulness we can muster, and each stage of our ongoing birth, and the confident joy of our inherent luminosity."

—Stephen Levine

Engage and Immerse: Breath-Focused Meditation (One to Five Minutes)

The breath-focused meditation is typically a short meditation intended to refocus you during your day. You can do this anytime, anywhere. I usually do it when I feel particularly stressed but don't have a lot of time to meditate.

Start by sitting in a comfortable position. Take a deep breath in and let it go, slowly, gently closing your eyes, then return to breathing normally. Take a few moments to notice how your body feels. Does it feel good? Are you sore anywhere? Tense anywhere? Once you've acknowledged these feelings, allow yourself to let them go. Softly pull your focus inward to your breath. Notice how each intake of air is different from the last. If you find yourself straying to other thoughts, gently let go of them, allow them to pass you by, and bring yourself back to the breath. Allow your breath to lead your mind instead of the other way around. Continue this for a few moments. When you're ready, slowly, gently open your eyes. Think of the blessings in your life, and continue your day with that sense of being blessed.

POWER THOUGHTS: A THANKFUL WAY OF LIFE

. . . .

"Gratitude and esteem are good foundations of affection."

—Jane Austen

. . . .

"When you arise in the morning, think of what a precious privilege it is to be alive—to breathe, to think, to enjoy, to love."

—Marcus Aurelius

"I have found that worry and irritation vanish the moment when I open my mind to the many blessing that I possess."

—Dale Carnegie

"It is impossible to feel grateful and depressed in the same moment."

—Naomi Williams

How You Can Have an Attitude of Gratitude

1. Be grateful and recognize the things others have done to help you.

2. When you say, "Thank you," to someone, it signals what you appreciate and why you appreciate it.

3. Post a "Thank you to all" on your Facebook page or in your blog, or send individual e-mails to friends, family, and colleagues.

4. Send a handwritten thank-you note. These are noteworthy because so few of us take the time to write and mail them.

5. Think thoughts of gratitude—about two or three good things that happened today—and notice the calm settling through your head, at least for a moment. You have activated a part of the brain that floods the body with endorphins, or feel-good hormones.

6. Remember the ways your life has been made easier or better because of others' efforts. Be aware of and acknowledge the good things, large and small, going on around you.

7. Keep a gratitude journal and set aside time each day or evening to list the people or things you're grateful for today. The list may start out short, but it will grow as you notice more of the good things around you.

8. Being grateful shakes you out of self-absorption and helps you recognize those who've done wonderful things for you. Expressing that gratitude continues to draw those people into your sphere.

9. Remember this thought from Maya Angelou: "When you learn, teach; when you get, give."

10. Join forces to do good. If you have survived illness or loss, you may want to reach out to others to help them, as a way of showing gratitude for those who reached out to you.

CHAPTER 2

MINDFULNESS MANTRAS

"Radiate boundless love toward the entire world."

—Buddha

Mindfulness is a word that for many has no real, solid definition. It's all well and good to talk about paying attention to the world around you, but in real life, how practical is that, really? After all, we live in a world where we're constantly connected—to work, to friends, even to that guy you met once in high school and who occasionally likes your tweets. What good is it to only sit and observe the places you go every day, when there's so much else going on that you could be missing?

As many of the people quoted in this book would tell you, practicing mindfulness really does do a lot of good. In an age when practically everyone is struggling with some level of anxiety and depression, mindfulness can help you refocus. It can remind you that you likely have everything you really need. And if you don't, practicing mindfulness can help you to accept the reality of where you are now, and help you move toward what you need, instead of allowing difficulties and hardships to bog you down.

Mindfulness is not a get-well-quick scheme. It's a new way of life.

"The essence of bravery is being without self-deception."

—Pema Chödrön

"Acknowledging the pain and the suffering that take place inside you, and allowing the feelings, will take time, but this new way of handling these feelings will change the way you relate to you and to the outside world."

—Kelly Martin

"In fact, when you're mindful, you actually feel irritation more keenly. However, once you unburden yourself from the delusion that people are deliberately trying to screw you, it's easier to stop getting carried away."

—Dan Harris

. . . .

*"By learning to allow different types of discomfort
to simply stay in the room with you, without
your scrambling for a button to push (real or
metaphorical), you make discomfort matter less.
The pool of things you're afraid of shrinks. It becomes
a lot less important to control circumstances, because
you know you can handle moments of uncertainty or
awkwardness or disappointment without an
escape plan."*

—David Cain

. . . .

*"By identifying impermanence as a fundamental
characteristic of existence itself, rather than a
problem to be solved, the Buddhists are encouraging
us to let go our hold on illusory solidity and learn to
swim freely in the sea of change."*

—Andrew Olendzki

Be a Buddha

So to be a human being is to be a Buddha.
Buddha nature is just another name
for human nature,
our true human nature. Thus even though
you do not do anything,
you are actually doing something.
You are expressing yourself.
You are expressing your true nature.
Your eyes will express;
your voice will express;
your demeanor will express.
The most important thing is to express
your true nature
in the simplest, most adequate way
and to appreciate it in the smallest existence.

—Shunryu Suzuki

POWER THOUGHTS: MINDFULNESS MANTRAS FROM THE MASTERS

. . . .

"Mindfulness is deliberately paying full attention to what is happening around you—in your body, heart, and mind. Mindfulness is awareness, without criticism or judgment."

—Hab Chozen Bays

. . . .

"Mindfulness has helped me succeed in almost every dimension of my life. By stopping regularly to look inward and become aware of my mental state, I stay connected to the source of my actions and thoughts, and can guide them with considerably more intention."

—Dustin Moskovitz

. . . .

"Paying attention to, and staying with finer and finer sensations within the body, is one of the surest ways to steady the wandering mind."

—Ravi Ravindra

"Sati—sampajanna ('*Mindfulness and clear comprehension*') *should be examined carefully from the point of view of the centipede who could not walk when she thought about how she moved her limbs. And also from the point of view of absorption in, say, artistic creation, and detached observation of it. Absorption in piano playing or painting seems to be 'successful,' but detached observation or enjoyment of 'my playing'...seems to have the centipede effect.*"

—Nanamoli Thera

"The most fundamental aggression to ourselves, the most fundamental harm we can do to ourselves, is to remain ignorant by not having the courage and the respect to look at ourselves honestly and gently."

—Pema Chödrön

Engage and Immerse: Quiet Observation Meditation (Five to Fifteen Minutes)

The quiet observation meditation is intended to bring you back to where you are and to what you already have, all round you. I use it when I want to remind myself of how much life has given me, and to appreciate it in a new and greater way.

Sit or stand in a maintainable, comfortable position. Begin by taking a deep breath in, and as you breathe out, slowly close your eyes. Take a few regular breaths and focus on your breathing, on how your body moves with each intake, on how your muscles soften each time you exhale. When you are ready, gently let go of that focus. Take a few moments to listen. What do you hear? Is there a faint buzzing from machinery? Can you hear the wind outside? Are people talking nearby? Be careful to observe your surroundings without judgment. When you are ready, open your eyes and slowly examine what you can see. Notice the details of every object around you. Acknowledge the existence of each and every thing that you can see and hear. When you have finished, let go of that observational focus, and mindfully resume your day.

"If you meditate in perfect peace, and then flash someone an irritable look because they make noise or their child cries, you are entirely missing the point."

—Khandro Rinpoche

"It stands to reason that anyone who learns to live well will die well. The skills are the same: being present in the moment, and humble, and brave, and keeping a sense of humor."

—Victoria Moran

"You can't stop the waves, but you can learn to surf."

—Jon Kabat-Zinn

"One does not become enlightened by imagining figures of light, but by making the darkness conscious. The latter procedure, however, is disagreeable and therefore not popular."

—C. G. Jung

"You might be tempted to avoid the messiness of daily living for the tranquility of stillness and peacefulness. This of course would be an attachment to stillness, and like any strong attachment, it leads to delusion. It arrests development and short-circuits the cultivation of wisdom."

—Jon Kabat-Zinn

"If you live the sacred and despise the ordinary, you are still bobbing in the ocean of delusion."

—Linji Yixuan

Learn as You Go: How Should I Sit When I Meditate?

When you meditate, you don't have to sit on the floor with your legs crossed in some amazingly flexible way. In fact, if you don't normally sit on the floor or cross your legs, you should avoid doing either of those things! Instead, you can sit on a chair in an easily maintainable position, your feet flat on the floor and your back straight, but not rigid. Meditation is supposed to help you, so it's important to set yourself up for success by sitting in a comfortable position.

· ·

"Feelings, whether of compassion or irritation, should be welcomed, recognized, and treated on an absolutely equal basis; because both are ourself. The tangerine I am eating is me. The mustard greens I am planting are me. I plant with all my heart and mind. I clean this teapot with the kind of attention I would have were I giving the baby Buddha or Jesus a bath. Nothing should be treated more carefully than anything else."

—Thích Nhất Hạnh

"In a true you-and-I relationship, we are present mindfully, nonintrusively, the way we are present with things in nature. We do not tell a birch tree it should be more like an elm. We face it with no agenda, only an appreciation that becomes participation: 'I love looking at this birch' becomes 'I am this birch,' and then 'I and this birch are opening to a mystery that transcends and holds us both.'"

—David Richo

"It takes a little bit of mindfulness and a little bit of attention to others to be a good listener, which helps cultivate emotional nurturing and engagement."

—Deepak Chopra

"With silence comes mindfulness, and thus we become better at choosing our words with kind intent before we express them."

—Alaric Hutchinson

"When you open your mind, you open new doors to new possibilities for yourself, and new opportunities to help others."

—Roy Bennett

· · · ·

"Respond; don't react.
Listen; don't talk.
Think; don't assume."

—Raji Lukkoor

· ·

"When you practice mindfulness, you bloom like
a flower."

—Debasish Mridha

CHAPTER 3

MASTER MINDFUL GRATITUDE, AND YOU WILL MASTER YOUR LIFE

"Mindfulness is both a state of mind and a skill."

—Renee Metty

People need mindfulness more than ever. The world has grown increasingly complicated and interdependent. The pace of life has accelerated tremendously and continues to move more and more quickly. Most people crave an antidote. Mindfulness provides a remedy. The practice of mindfulness simplifies, creates calm, and offers new ways to navigate the churning, uncharted waters of our modern age. What exactly is mindfulness, one may wonder? Although it's a popular term, pinpointing the exact definition of mindfulness can be difficult. Do I have to get up early? Must I do some special ritual? Mindfulness has always been something simple, yet quite profound. Mindfulness in its essence means paying attention.

Mindfulness appears to be a straightforward process. Essentially it is. Yet because life holds enormous potential for complication, continued practice and mastery of mindfulness can be challenging. There are so many distractions that can make paying attention a problematic venture, and therein lies the paradox of mindfulness. There are mundane distractions, such as to-do lists, a pile of laundry, or a pebble in your shoe. There are more monumental distractions, such as natural disasters, death, accidents, or other big life changes. Mindfulness, as a practice, offers tips and tools to stay present, focused, and relaxed through it all, big and small.

The daily requirements of mindfulness depend on the conditions of the day. Just as a surfer must stay present, prepared, and ready to jump into action to catch a wave, a mindfulness practitioner must remain poised and ready to move with whatever influx life presents. Sometimes the waves are small, so we need to train our attention so we don't become bored. Sometimes the waves seem huge and impassable. In that case, we may need to focus on our own inner fear to get through the surf conditions of the day. Mindfulness offers us ideas and insight for staying present and alert through it all.

The Contemplation on No-Coming and No-Going

This body is not me.
I am not limited by this body.
I am life without boundaries.
I have never been born,
and I have never died.
Look at the ocean and the sky filled with stars,
manifestations from my wondrous true mind.
Since before time, I have been free.
Birth and death are only doors
through which we pass,
sacred thresholds on our journey.
Birth and death are a game of hide-and-seek.
So laugh with me,
hold my hand,
let us say goodbye,
say goodbye, to meet again soon.
We meet today.
We will meet again tomorrow.
We will meet at the source every moment.
We meet each other in all forms of life.

—Thích Nhất Hạnh

Blessing of All the Buddhas

O Guru Rinpoche, Precious One,
You are the embodiment of
The compassion and blessings of all the buddhas,
The only protector of beings.
My body, my possessions, my heart and soul
Without hesitation, I surrender to you!
From now until I attain enlightenment,
In happiness or sorrow,
in circumstances good or bad,
in situations high or low:
I rely on you completely, O Padmasambhava,
you who know me:
think of me, inspire me, guide me,
make me one with you!

—Jikmé Lingpa, excerpt from
The Tibetan Book of Living and Dying

Power Thoughts: Be Here Now, Always

. . . .

"Replace fear of your own inner experience, with a curious, gentle, welcoming attitude—free of judgment, self-blame, and aversion."

—Melanie Greenberg

. . . .

"Mindfulness shows us what is happening in our bodies, our emotions, our minds, and in the world. Through mindfulness, we avoid harming ourselves and others."

—Thích Nhất Hạnh

"Mindful self-compassion can be learned by anyone. It's the practice of repeatedly evoking good will toward ourselves, especially when we're suffering— cultivating the same desire that all living beings have to live happily and free from suffering."

—Christopher Germer

"Mindfulness: Taking a balanced approach to negative emotions, so that feelings are neither suppressed nor exaggerated. We cannot ignore our pain and feel compassion for it at the same time. Mindfulness requires that we not 'over-identify' with thoughts and feelings, so that we are caught up and swept away by negativity."

—Brené Brown

. . . .

"It's not that God, the environment, and other people cannot help us to be happy or find satisfaction. It's just that our happiness, satisfaction, and our understanding, even of God, will be no deeper than our capacity to know ourselves inwardly, to encounter the world from the deep comfort that comes from being at home in one's own skin, from an intimate familiarity with the ways of one's own mind and body."

—Jon Kabat-Zinn

Power Practice: Ritual Purification

Many religions and cultures have their own forms of ritual cleansings (baptisms/christening, mikveh, ghusl/wudu, snanam, etc.), each with different symbolism. Though many of these rituals are purely spiritual, some also incorporate material objects for both physical and metaphysical cleansing. For instance, the Romans used oils and fragrances, the Indians used herbs and spices, and even Cleopatra added milk and honey to her baths. These rituals are typically used to mark a rebirth or significant change in one's life, and are often believed to have purifying properties. While some of these ancient rituals have come under criticism by women for suggesting that women are unclean, modern feminists have reclaimed spiritual bathing as a way to appreciate femininity and oneself. Any woman can incorporate the idea of ritual cleansing into their life, in a variety of forms, either similar or symbolic to the original concepts. Taking a meditative bath with your favorite oils and candles, cleaning out your house, or even deleting toxic friends from social media can all be compared to the cleansing and rebirth that is at the core of these ritual ceremonies.

⸘ Present Moment Practice

A daily practice that calms my body and centers my mind is *"abhyanga,"* a mindful practice based in Ayurveda that means "self-massage." In traditional abhyanga, one uses oil, such as sesame or coconut oil, sometimes infused with essential oils. Abhyanga can be as simple as massaging your own hands or feet or the entire body. The importance of abhyanga comes from its link to compassion. When we treat ourselves kindly, the rewards are great. I find that abhyanga helps me to be more self-reliant and proactive. I am taking care of myself through my own sense of loving touch and mindful self-care. When I care for myself with my own hands, I take time to reflect on the sacredness and importance of me right now. I pay careful attention and am mindful of my own body and health. This is one of my favorite mindful practices.

POWER THOUGHTS: STAYING GROUNDED IN THE PRESENT MOMENT

. . . .

"If we could see the miracle of a single flower clearly, our whole life would change."

—Buddha

. . . .

"The skill of mindfulness allows you to remain grounded in the present moment, even when you face difficult stressors, so that your stressful feelings feel more manageable."

—Melanie Greenberg

"Mindfulness means being present to whatever is happening here and now—when mindfulness is strong, there is no room left in the mind for wanting something else. With less liking and disliking of what arises, there is less pushing and pulling on the world, less defining of the threshold between self and other, resulting in a reduced construction of self. As the influence of self diminishes, suffering diminishes in proportion."

—Andrew Olendzki

"In meditation, we discover our inherent restlessness. Sometimes we get up and leave. Sometimes we sit there, but our bodies wiggle and squirm, and our minds go far away. This can be so uncomfortable that we feel it's impossible to stay. Yet this feeling can teach us not just about ourselves, but what it is to be human... We really don't want to stay with the nakedness of our present experience."

—Pema Chödrön

"It's like wearing gloves every time we touch something, and then, forgetting we chose to put them on, we complain that nothing feels quite real. Our challenge each day is not to get dressed to face the world, but to un-love ourselves, so that the doorknob feels cold, and the car handle feels wet, and the kiss goodbye feels like the lips of another being, soft and unrepeatable."

—Mark Nepo

"There is something wonderfully bold and liberating about saying yes to our entire imperfect and messy life."

—Tara Brach

"Sit back and enjoy your problems."

—Marina Diamandis

Learn as You Go: How Long Should I Meditate For?

You may have noticed that each "Engage and Immerse" meditation has a suggested amount of time in parentheses next to the title. These are merely suggestions, to give you an idea of how long each meditation may take when you start. That being said, you can meditate for as long or as little as you want. Do you only have two minutes to meditate on your break? Meditate for two minutes. Do you want to meditate for an hour before or after work? Meditate for an hour. Meditation is ultimately for your well-being, so you get to decide how long you do it.

THERE IS NO PAST; THERE IS NO FUTURE—ONLY NOW

. . . .

"Do not dwell in the past; do not dream of the future; concentrate the mind on the present moment."

—Buddha

. . . .

"Start living right here, in each present moment. When we stop dwelling on the past or worrying about the future, we're open to rich sources of information we've been missing out on—information that can keep us out of the downward spiral, and poised for a richer life."

—Mark Williams

"What is the date? What is the time?... Great, that's what Now is. And every second, your 'now' changes. Because all we have is Now. We are continuously living in the Now. Not yesterday, not tomorrow, but Now. Today. the present. And I need you to live in it. To truly appreciate it. To breathe and feel yourself breathing."

—S.R. Crawford

"It goes against the grain to stay present. These are the times when only gentleness and a sense of humor can give us the strength to settle down... So whenever we wander off, we gently encourage ourselves to 'stay' and settle down. Are we experiencing restlessness? Stay! Are fear and loathing out of control? Stay! Aching knees and throbbing back? Stay! What's for lunch? Stay! I can't stand this another minute! Stay!"

—Pema Chödrön

"We have only now, only this single eternal moment opening and unfolding before us, day and night."

—Jack Kornfield

"If you are doing mindfulness meditation, you are doing it with your ability to attend to the moment."

—Daniel Goleman

Engage and Immerse: Mindful Eating Meditation (Ten to Twenty Minutes)

The mindful eating meditation is intended to help you to become mindful in your day-to-day activities and tasks. I especially like to do this meditation when I've had a day full of planning or worrying about the future, because it grounds me back into the present.

This meditation can be done during a meal or a snack, which should be prepared before you start. Begin by taking a deep breath in and letting it out, drawing your mind to the present moment and each individual action you take during it. Then you may start to eat your meal. As you eat, focus on exactly what you're doing while you're doing it. If you have to open a container, acknowledge the container, pay attention to the action of opening it. If you are using utensils, notice the feel of the utensils in your hands, the weight and motion of rising and falling when you bring food from the dish to your mouth. With each bite, savor the flavors and textures of the food. Allow them to be what they are, without judging them. It does not matter whether you like or dislike what you are eating—either way, the food will sustain you. Continue this meditation until you have finished eating.

CHAPTER 4

GRATITUDE FOR THE LITTLE THINGS ALL AROUND YOU

"Every experience, no matter how bad it seems, holds within it a blessing of some kind. The goal is to find it."

—Buddha

This is your life; only you can truly control your choices, and choosing thankfulness and happiness is the best way to achieve being good to yourself as well as to the world. Here are some suggestions for how you can ensure simple joy in your life:

- Be the best you can be, by your own standards.
- Surround yourself with people who inspire you and make you feel good.
- Focus on what you have, not what you lack.
- Optimism trumps pessimism every time!
- Smile often and genuinely.
- Be honest, to yourself and to others.
- Help others.
- Embrace your past, live in the present, and look forward for what is yet to come.

And here is a really bold idea about embracing mindful gratitude: unplug (and recharge!).

Forego using technological devices today. Texting your friend, watching your favorite show, checking your email—all can wait until tomorrow! Turn off your devices and turn on your senses! Read a book, cook a meal, and enjoy the outdoors by taking a walk or tending to your garden. Technology distracts us from the real world, occupying our attention with game applications, chat rooms, social media websites, commercials, and so on. Want to know what's going on in the news? Read a newspaper. Be aware of the here and now by finding activities that don't require electricity or a battery. Meditate.

> *"Each step along the Buddha's path to happiness requires practicing mindfulness, until it becomes part of your daily life."*

—Henepola Gunaratana

> *"Our culture encourages us to plan every moment, and fill our schedules with one activity and obligation after the next, with no time to just be. But the human body and mind require downtime to rejuvenate. I have found my greatest moments of joy and peace just sitting in silence, and then I take that joy and peace with me out into the world."*

—Holly Mosier

"Be happy in the moment, that's enough. Each moment is all we need, not more."

—Mother Teresa

"This is the real secret of life—to be completely engaged with what you are doing in the here and now. And instead of calling it work, realize it is play."

—Alan Watts

Learn the Language of Kindness: Love Is Love Is Gratitude

I learned from my globetrotting friend, Santosh, that one of the nicest things a traveler can do is to learn how to say the basics in the language of the locals. He stressed that saying "thank you" is the *most* important word of all. His guide to global gratitude is below:

Czech: Děkuji

Danish: Tak

Dutch: Dank u

Estonian: Tänan teid

Filipino: Salamat

Finnish: Kiitos

French: Merci

Gaelic: Go raibh maith agat

German: Danke

Hungarian: Köszönöm

Indonesian: Terima kasih

Italian: Grazie

Japanese: Arigato

Latvian: Paldies

Norwegian: Takk

Polish: Dziękuję

Portuguese: Obrigado

Romanian: Mulțumesc

Spanish: Gracias

Swahili: Asante

Swedish: Tack

Vietnamese: Cảm ơn bạn

Welsh: Diolch yn fawr

Learn as You Go: When and Where Should I Meditate?

As you may already know, meditation can be done anytime and anywhere. That being said, if you want to build a lasting habit, you should try to meditate at approximately the same time and place each day. This way, your brain will start to associate that time and place with meditating and will be prepared when you get there.

"To be sensual, I think, is to respect and rejoice in the force of life, of life itself, and to be present in all that one does, from the effort of loving, to the breaking of bread."

—James Baldwin

"The present moment is filled with joy and happiness. If you are attentive, you will see it."

—Thích Nhất Hạnh

"The only way to live is by accepting each minute as an unrepeatable miracle."

—Tara Brach

"The things that matter most in our lives are not fantastic or grand. They are moments when we touch one another."

—Jack Kornfield

"The moment one gives close attention to anything, even a blade of grass, it becomes a mysterious, awesome, indescribably magnificent world in itself."

—Henry Miller

"Seek and see all the marvels around you. You will get tired of looking at yourself alone, and that fatigue will make you deaf and blind to everything else."

—Don Juan

Engage and Immerse: Nature-Focused Meditative Walk (Five to Fifteen Minutes)

The nature-focused meditative walk is intended to remind you of all the natural beauty that exists around you every day. I like to do it whenever I've spend much of the day (or the week) inside, especially if I've been focused primarily on difficult tasks or complaints.

Begin by standing still outside. Take a deep breath in and let it out, then take your first step, walking and breathing normally, not too fast and not too slow. As you walk, take notice of your surroundings. Look for pockets of nature—is grass peeking through the cracks in the sidewalk? Are there trees and bushes anywhere? How about flowers? Look for green plants, brown earth, blue or gray sky. Is it cold or warm? Bright or cloudy? Continue your walk and observe your surroundings without judging them: let them be what they are.

"Life is not lost by dying; life is lost minute by minute, day by dragging day, in all the small uncaring ways."

—Stephen Vincent Benet

"Mindfulness helps us freeze the frame, so that we can become aware of our sensations and experiences as they are, without the distorting coloration of socially conditioned responses or habitual reactions."

—Henepola Gunaratana

"Rejoicing in ordinary things is not sentimental or trite. It actually takes guts."

—Pema Chödrön

"It's a funny thing about life, once you begin to take note of the things you are grateful for, you begin to lose sight of the things that you lack."

—Germany Kent

"Looking at beauty in the world is the first step of purifying the mind."

—Amit Ray

How Thank-You Notes Can Change the World

Write a note of gratitude, a "mindful memo," to the people in your everyday life who make a difference—the mailman, a grocery clerk, or the greeter at the mall. Tell your friends about their places of business or their great service so their businesses can grow. Just by paying attention to those people in your everyday life who can so easily go unnoticed (especially if your smartphone is glued to your hand), you can enrich each other's life a little each day.

Chapter 5

Simple Wisdom: Practice Mindfulness with Understanding and Intentionality

Mindfulness is more than just looking around you and noticing things, like the color of the walls and the feel of the chair beneath you. Mindfulness is intentionally focusing on where you are and what you're doing right now, and it's done in the small moments. Do you have a scary doctor's appointment tomorrow? Force yourself to focus on the work you're doing now. Are you distracted by Facebook while eating dinner? Put the phone down and enjoy your meal; pay attention to the unique flavors and textures of the food. Instead of waking up and immediately picking up your phone or starting your morning routine, take three minutes to sit, to breathe, to start the day right. Allow yourself time to just *be*.

Meditation—the act of sitting and focusing on your breathing, of letting go of your thoughts and life for just a few minutes of your day—can help you to start living with mindfulness, to start living here and now instead of next week and online. But true mindfulness happens when you're actively living life—when you're going about your day. As you travel to work, keep your phone in your pocket, and notice the things which you don't normally pay attention to. What stores are around you at the stoplight? Is there a secret park somewhere that you never knew about? Is the sun warm and the sky blue, or is it cloudy and cold? Look around without judging. Will complaining internally about the winter cold make the earth tilt back toward the sun? Of course not. Accept the reality of what is.

Don't stop with your surroundings, though. Also pay attention to what's happening in your own heart and mind. Allow things to be what they are. When you're happy, hold on to the emotion and really feel it. When you're sad or stressed, allow yourself to be sad or stressed. Acknowledge the hardships you're facing, instead of trying to push them deep down inside the dark corners of your heart. If you can allow reality to be what it is, if you can allow yourself to be who you are, you can learn how to accept anger and sadness, and then let it go.

Start by giving yourself a few moments every day to pay attention to what's around and inside you. If you can, do this at the same time every day. Be intentional. Build a habit. Soon, you'll find that you're able to focus a little more easily on what you're working. You'll find yourself enjoying the small, individual moments that make each day unique. And you'll be able to let go of things you never thought you could just let go of.

"Three things cannot be long hidden: the sun, the moon, and the truth."

—Buddha

"Wherever you decide to go, proceed with your mind."

—Amitav Chowdhury

"The key to creating the mental space before responding is mindfulness. Mindfulness is a way of being present: paying attention to and accepting what is happening in our lives. It helps us to be aware of and step away from our automatic and habitual reactions to our everyday experiences."

—Elizabeth Thornton

"Everything is created twice, first in the mind, and then in reality."

—Roshan Sharma

"Buddhist mindfulness is about the present, but I also think it's about being real. Being awake to everything. Feeling like nothing can hurt you if you can look it straight on."

—Krista Tippett

"If someone comes along and shoots an arrow into your heart, it's fruitless to stand there and yell at the person. It would be much better to turn your attention to the fact that there's an arrow in your heart."

—Pema Chödrön

Learn as You Go: How Often Should I Meditate?

If you're trying to build a habit and improve your mindfulness, you should meditate at least once a day. However, if that is too stressful, don't force it! Like I've said before, meditating is your tool—if you can't meditate every day, do it when you can, so you don't lose the benefits. Of course, there's no need to limit yourself to meditating only once per day—feel free to do it as often as you want to.

. . . .

"In any moment of time, you have three paths to choose from. You stand for something, you stand against something, or you drop both, and walk with your inner truth."

—Roshan Sharma

. . . .

"We need never be bound by the limitations of our previous or current thinking, nor are we ever locked into being the person we used to be, or think we are."

—Allan Lokos

. . . .

"Open the window of your mind. Allow the fresh air, new lights, and new truths to enter."

—Amit Ray

"Mindfulness isn't about ridding yourself of thoughts. It's more about being aware and letting those thoughts pass through you, so you can see what, if any, value they have for you. Thoughts are an illusion but some of them are enlightening."

—Nanette Mathews

"Think of the old cliché about the mind being 'an excellent servant but a terrible master.' This, like many clichés, so lame and banal on the surface, actually expresses a great and terrible truth."

—David Foster Wallace

Engage and Immerse: Inward-Focused Meditative Walk (Five to Six Minutes)

The inward-focused meditative walk is intended to use the movement of your body while walking as a focus for your mind. I like to do it when I've been sitting still all day, when sitting more to meditate is difficult and distraction-filled.

Begin by standing still in a safe location. Take a deep breath in and allow your eyes to slowly close as you breathe out, then breathe normally. Focus on the weight of your body transferring to the ground. Notice the small movements you normally make without thinking about them, the shifts that help you maintain balance. Once you feel grounded, slowly open your eyes and take your first step. Walk normally—not too slow, not too fast. As you begin walking, focus on the sensations of your feet as they meet the ground. Notice how your weight transfers, the textures that rub against each foot as you take a step. When you're ready, slowly bring your focus upward to your legs. Notice how your ankles and knees are bending, how your leg muscles expand and contract. How the fabric around your legs feels as it shifts along with your pace. When you're ready, raise your focus to your torso. Pay attention to the small twists and turns it makes as you're walking, to the weight of your top on your body. Over time, expand this focus to include your arms. Are they swinging? If so, how far? Do they feel heavy or light? When you feel content with how you have acknowledged and appreciated each part of your body, shift your focus to your head. Notice how you're holding it and release any tension in your neck or in the rest of your body. Allow yourself to relax and enjoy the walk. When you're ready, gently let go of your inward focus and continue with your day.

"Use every distraction as an object of meditation, and they cease to be distractions."

—Mingyur Rinpoche

"You must have hope in a better future and have faith in this hope. But then you must forget your hope and focus on this moment now."

—Kamand Kojouri

"Reality is only an agreement—today is always today."

—Zen Proverb

"The mind is capable of the highest wisdom. It can experience love and compassion, as well as anger. It can understand history, philosophy, and mathematics—and also remember what's on the grocery list. The mind is truly like a wish-fulfilling jewel. With an untrained mind, the thought process is said to be like a wild and blind horse: erratic and out of control."

—Sakyong Mipham

"Knowledge does not mean mastering a great quantity of different information, but understanding the nature of mind. This knowledge can penetrate each one of our thoughts, and illuminate each one of our perceptions."

—Matthieu Ricard

Don't Just Go Through It, Grow Through It

An attitude of gratitude can make a profound difference in our day-to-day lives, yet, as we all come to know, not every day is filled with all good things. We each endure difficult passages: illnesses, money trouble, work woes, relationship issues, the loss of a loved one, and countless others. These are the vicissitudes of life. However, it is the attitude you bring to each situation that makes all the difference. Share the life lessons that you learned from others, if you think they can help a fellow traveler who is walking a hard path.

CHAPTER 6

TO BE MINDFUL IS TO BE OBJECTIVE, NON-JUDGMENTAL

It's easy to judge others for their actions, and take for granted those we love or meet in chance encounters. We sometimes get so caught up in our own busy-ness, that we forget others are busy, too; they have rough days just like us, and they benefit from our kindnesses, just as we do from theirs. Go out of your way to smile at strangers, say good morning, say thank you, give a compliment, and listen attentively to someone who needs your ear. Do it because you can, because it feels great, because it makes someone else feel good. Don't worry about a subsequent thank you; let a thank you be a beautiful perk, rather than an expectation.

"Whatever you did today is enough. Whatever you felt today is valid. Whatever you thought today isn't to be judged. Repeat the above each day."

—Brittany Burgunder

"Happiness or sorrow—whatever befalls you, walk on untouched, unattached."

—Buddha

"Central to our work and our goal of finding solutions to global problems is the concept of mindfulness, a technique for focusing attention objectively on the here and now."

—Goldie Hawn

· · · · · · · · · · · · · · · · · · ·

"Mindfulness is simply being aware of what is happening right now without wishing it were different, enjoying the pleasant without holding on when it changes (which it will), being with the unpleasant without fearing it will always be this way (which it won't)."

—James Baraz

"As we encounter new experiences with a mindful and wise attention, we discover that one of three things will happen to our new experience: it will go away, it will stay the same, or it will get more intense. Whatever happens does not really matter."

—Jack Kornfield

". . . . ."

"The ultimate experience of being mindful occurs when we forget about everything, even the mindful self and doing. In that mode we are full of energy, utterly self-generated."

—Sang H. Kim

". . . . ."

"Mindfulness is wordless. Mindfulness is meeting the moment as it is, moment after moment after moment, wordlessly attending to our experiencing as it actually is. It is opening to not just the fragments of our lives that we like or dislike or view as important, but the whole of our experiencing."

—White Wind Zen Community

Learn as You Go: What Expectations Should I Have for Meditation?

None! If you go into meditation with fixed expectations, you may feel pressured in a way that meditation cannot help. Since everyone is different, everyone will have different results from meditation, and that's okay. But it's important not to have too many expectations, because if you are too dissatisfied with your results, you may overlook the small, day-to-day improvements that meditation is helping you make.

"The best way to capture moments is to pay attention. This is how we cultivate mindfulness."

—Jon Kabat-Zinn

"Mindfulness is living in the moment without judging it."

—Debasish Mridha

"Being mindful means that we suspend judgment for a time, set aside our immediate goals for the future, and take in the present moment as it is, rather than as we would like it to be."

—Mark Williams

"Nowadays, mindfulness has become a catch-all word, but the general principle of trying to be more conscious and aware in our daily life is very important. Along with this, it's helpful to contemplate some of the mind training verses which are designed to take and transform all of the problems we experience."

—Tenzin Palmo

"Most of us take for granted that time flies, meaning that it passes too quickly. But in the mindful state, time doesn't really pass at all. There is only a single instant of time that keeps renewing itself over and over with infinite variety."

—Deepak Chopra

Engage and Immerse: Day Scan Meditation (Five to Six Minutes)

The day scan meditation is intended to help you process your day and prepare for sleep. I especially like to do this meditation after a long, exhausting day, or perhaps after a day when I've felt particularly unproductive or felt I failed at a goal I'd been working toward for a while.

Begin this meditation in your bed, in the same position in which you intend to fall asleep. Take a deep breath in, a deep breath out, and as you exhale, gently close your eyes. For a moment, focus on your breathing only. Prepare yourself to observe without judgment, to recap without having any opinion. Remember that you want to go through your entire day in five or six minutes. Then begin. Start with the morning routine, remembering this morning's unique occurrences, and continue quickly through the rest of the day. Remember that you are not in a rush; rather, you are merely acknowledging the day's events. So you do not want to spend too much time on anything, you don't want to give yourself time to judge it or wallow in it. The purpose of this meditation is not to dwell on the day's hardships or joys, but rather to allow them to have been, to allow them to have had meaning in their moments, to process them, and then to let go.

"What I must do is all that concerns me, not what the people think. This rule, equally arduous in actual and in intellectual life, may serve for the whole distinction between greatness and meanness. It is the harder, because you will always find those who think they know what is your duty better than you know it."

—Ralph Waldo Emerson

"Mindfulness is the aware, balanced acceptance of the present experience. It isn't more complicated than that. It is opening to or receiving the present moment, pleasant or unpleasant, just as it is, without either clinging to it or rejecting it."

—Sylvia Boorstein

. . . .

"Mindfulness is like a microscope; it is neither an offensive nor defensive weapon in relation to the germs we observe through it. The function of the microscope is just to clearly present what is there."

—Chogyam Trungpa

"Mindfulness is the act of being intensely aware of what you're sensing and feeling at every moment—without interpretation or judgment."

—Mayo Clinic

"Suffering usually relates to wanting things to be different than they are."

—Allan Lokos

CHAPTER 7

THE PRACTICE OF INTENTIONAL AWARENESS

"We are alive in the present moment, the only moment there is for us to be alive."

—**Thích Nhất Hạnh**

Mindfulness can refer to paying attention to the present moment, or it can describe meditation, as in mindfulness meditation. Open your eyes to practice mindfulness as a state of mind or close your eyes to develop the skill of meditation.

With our eyes shut, we practice mindful meditation. Mindful meditation can be practiced sitting in silence and focusing on the breath. Thoughts interrupt the practice of doing nothing; the meditator continues the practice of staying present and not distracted. Mindful meditation helps a person to harness the mind and sharpen focus, and it prepares one for staying present and attentive in daily life.

Think of the following metaphor. If life is a big party, the meditation part becomes the pre-party preparation. We clean, we organize, we plan the activities and the guest list. We get ready for the big party. Meditation becomes a way to prepare to be in the present moment for the party. We organize, sort through our thoughts, and clear the mind to make space for life.

Then on the day of the party, we engage in what I call "everyday mindfulness." We practice being present and engaged, having fun, or maybe not so much fun, as the party unfolds in whatever way it unfolds. We stay awake and fully connected.

"Everyday mindfulness" doesn't require shutting your eyes. All that's needed is the focus to engage in whatever is happening around you—to see, feel, smell, notice your body, taste, and listen. You can engage in mindful walking, dancing, gardening, or just watching clouds float by. Everyday mindfulness might be washing the dishes and feeling the warm water, the soap, the sponge, the grime, and the grease. It's a reckoning and surrender to the mundane.

In goal-oriented activities, mindfulness means paying attention in the moment and letting go of the outcome. For this reason, more and more professional and nonprofessional athletes are embracing the tenets and philosophies of mindfulness. We are better players in sports and in life when we live mindfully. The Golden State Warriors won two NBA championships in part by embracing a mission based on mindfulness.

If we take the practice of everyday mindfulness, focusing on what's happening around us, and relate it back to our short and long-term goals, we approach intentional awareness. Once we can clearly take in and face our present situation, we can make effective decisions that benefit what we hope to accomplish. In the short term, we take the present conditions, and channel them into our goals. Rather than going through life in autopilot mode, we respond to our present situation intentionally. In the long term, we can practice intentional awareness by planning our time and actions in accordance to our future goals.

"To enjoy good health, to bring true happiness to one's family, to bring peace to all, one must first discipline and control one's own mind."

—Buddha

"The art of living...is neither careless drifting on the one hand nor fearful clinging to the past on the other. It consists in being sensitive to each moment, in regarding it as utterly new and unique, in having the mind open and wholly receptive."

—Alan Watts

"Mindful awareness, as we will see, actually involves more than just simply being aware: It involves being aware of aspects of the mind itself. Instead of being on automatic and mindless, mindfulness helps us awaken, and by reflecting on the mind we are enabled to make choices, and thus change becomes possible."

—Daniel J. Siegel

"Mindfulness isn't just about knowing that you're hearing something, seeing something, or even observing that you're having a particular feeling. It's about doing so in a certain way—with balance and equanimity, and without judgment. Mindfulness is the practice of paying attention in a way that creates space for insight."

—Sharon Salzberg

"Every time we become aware of a thought, as opposed to being lost in a thought, we experience that opening of the mind."

—Joseph Goldstein

"The purpose of meditation practice is not enlightenment; it is to pay attention even at unextraordinary times, to be of present, nothing-but-the-present, to bear this mindfulness of now into each event of ordinary life."

—Peter Matthiessen

Learn as You Go: Do I Have to Meditate the Same Way Every Day?

The short answer: no, you do not. There's a reason why there are so many different types of meditation. Each day is unique, so you may find that being flexible in how you meditate will help you to get the most out of the practice. However, you may also find that you gravitate toward the same kind of meditation every day, and that's okay, too. Each person is different, so each person's meditative practices will look different.

> *"Mindfulness means paying attention in a particular way, on purpose, in the present moment, and nonjudgmentally."*
>
> —Jon Kabat-Zinn

> *"As with any form of mental self-improvement, you must learn to turn your gaze inward, concentrate on processes that usually run automatically, and try to wrest control of them so that you can apply them more mindfully."*
>
> —Steven Pinker

· ·

"In Tibet, we have a traditional image, the wind horse, which represents a balanced relationship between the wind and the mind. The horse represents wind and movement. On its saddle rides a precious jewel. That jewel is our mind... We experience the mind as moving all the time—suddenly darting off, thinking about one thing and another, being happy, being sad. If we haven't trained our mind, the wild horse takes us wherever it wants to go."

—Sakyong Mipham

"Say that the moment is a combination of thought; sensation; the voice of the sea. Waste, deadness, come from the inclusion of things that don't belong to the moment; this appalling narrative business of the realist: getting on from lunch to dinner: it is false, unreal, merely conventional."

—Virginia Woolf

"Practice is this life, and realization is this life, and this life is revealed right here and now."

—Maezumi Roshi

"*Tethered to our smart phones, we are too caught up and distracted to take the time necessary to sort through complexity or to locate submerged purpose. In our urgent rush to get 'there,' we are going everywhere but being nowhere. Far too busy managing with transactive speed, we rarely step back to lead with transformative significance.*"

—Kevin Cashman

Engage and Immerse: Mantra Meditation (Five to Twenty Minutes)

Mantra meditation is intended to use sounds, words, and phrases to refocus you. I like to do mantra meditation when I can't seem to escape all of my thoughts and worries about the future or the past.

For this meditation, you must come up with a word or phrase that you will repeat over and over again. This will be your mantra. One of the traditional words used is *Om* but it could be anything, secular or non, spiritual or non. Remember, though, that the word, sound, or phrase you use will replace your thoughts, so it should be chosen carefully, as it will be your focus for the entirety of your meditation and perhaps even for a period afterwards.

Begin by sitting in a comfortable position. Take a deep breath in, and let it out, slowly closing your eyes or allowing your visual focus to blur. Then begin your mantra. Repeat your chosen mantra slowly in your mind. You can repeat it silently or murmur or whisper it quietly out loud. Focus all of your mind, all of your energy, on your mantra, allowing it to consume your every thought. You can do this a certain number of times, using a method to track your number that does not involve focusing on counting, such as moving beads along a necklace. Or, you can do this for a set amount of time, setting a non-obtrusive, mild timer that will alert you to when your meditation is finished. When you are done, take a deep breath in, and as you let it out, allow yourself to refocus on the world around you, and mindfully continue your day.

"When you do something, you should burn yourself up completely, like a good bonfire, leaving no trace of yourself."

—Shunryu Suzuki

"Do not force your mind to get rid of random thoughts, because your brain is simply not capable of doing so. Instead, when you sit to practice meditation, let the thoughts come and go, just don't serve them tea. Over time, that background noise inside your head will disappear."

—Abhijit Naskar

"Meditation is a microcosm, a model, a mirror. The skills we practice when we sit are transferable to the rest of our lives."

—Sharon Salzberg

"What you feed your mind, will lead your life."

—Kemi Sogunle

"Mindfulness means being aware of how you're deploying your attention and making decisions about it, and not letting the tweet or the buzzing...call your attention."

—Howard Rheingold

"The mind is just like a muscle—the more you exercise it, the stronger it gets and the more it can expand."

—Idowu Koyenikan

"The body benefits from movement, and the mind benefits from stillness."

—Sakyong Mipham

Chapter 8

Peace in Every Breath and Every Step

My daily practice goes something like this. Almost without exception, I meditate daily. Most days I meditate for twenty minutes, sometimes less, sometimes more. The important thing for me is to do it daily. Consistency is a key. I believe that making mediation a daily habit is more important than the total duration of time sitting in silence. Later, after tea and other self-care practices, I take a mindful walk with my dog. Pets can be a great contribution to a mindful life. For me, I have found having a dog helps me to be more consistent in my focus and mindful of the time passing during the day. Dogs live mindfully and in tune with nature! All animals live mindfully, for they only know the present moment. Although they sometimes eat too quickly, they know when they are hungry and let us know. Many people believe they are too busy to care for an animal. I would say this might be exactly the reason to get one. Pets force us to slow down. They motivate us to walk and spend time in nature. I often listen to podcasts while walking my dog. However, I try to walk at least three times a week in silence, taking in the world around me with my senses. I smell the scents around me on my mindful walk. I feel my feet hitting the ground, and I notice my body and how it moves in space. I look at the light and see all the colors around me. I sometimes even try to taste the air, if it is pleasant. The more one taps into the senses, the more present one becomes.

Animals also teach us about compassion. They love unconditionally. Have you noticed that it is hard to live in the moment and be self-critical? Compassion and curiosity are essential factors of living in the moment. If I find myself upset, frustrated, or angry, I slow down and try to process. I may try some gentle or restorative yoga, especially on days when there is a lot to sort out. If I feel particularly overwhelmed, I sit down and meditate again.

. . . .

"Peace comes from within. Do not seek it without."

—Buddha

. . . .

"Mindfulness meditation doesn't change life. Life remains as fragile and unpredictable as ever. Meditation changes the heart's capacity to accept life as it is. It teaches the heart to be more accommodating, not by beating it into submission, but by making it clear that accommodation is a gratifying choice."

—Sylvia Boorstein

. . . .

"The practice of mindfulness begins in the small remote cave of your unconscious mind, and blossoms with the sunlight of your conscious life, reaching far beyond the people and places you can see."

—Earon Davis

"Step outside for a while—calm your mind. It is better to hug a tree than to bang your head against a wall continually."

—Rasheed Ogunlaru

"When you focus and accept the current moment with love, faith, and joyfulness, you are practicing mindfulness. That is better than controlling the universe."

—Debasish Mridha

"Eventually it will become quiet enough so that you can simply watch the heart begin to react, and let go before the mind starts. At some point in the journey it all becomes heart, not mind... The mind doesn't even get a chance to start up, because you let go at the heart level."

—Michael Singer

Learn as You Go: Do I Have to Close My Eyes When I Meditate?

Many people, especially at first, find that closing their eyes during meditation can help them to avoid distractions. Most of the meditations in this book, therefore, begin with having you close your eyes, even if just for a moment. However, if you find that you are able to focus without closing your eyes, feel free to keep them open.

"Your vision will become clear only when you look into your heart. Who looks outside, dreams. Who looks inside, awakens."

—Carl Jung

"Rather than fretting about the past or worrying about the future, the aim is to experience life as it unfolds moment by moment. This simple practice is immensely powerful. As we rush through our lives, mindfulness encourages us to stop constantly striving for something new or better, and to embrace acceptance and gratitude. This allows us to tap into the joy and wonder in our lives, and to listen to the wisdom of our hearts."

—Anna Barnes

. . . .

"In the end, just three things matter:
How well we have lived
How well we have loved
How well we have learned to let go."

—Jack Kornfield

. . . .

"Sometimes you need to sit lonely on the floor in a
quiet room in order to hear your own voice and not let
it drown in the noise of others."

—Charlotte Eriksson

Engage and Immerse: Loving Kindness Meditation (Ten to Twenty Minutes)

The loving kindness meditation is intended to draw your heart into your meditation and to show love toward everyone, yourself included. I like to do it when I've had a day full of irritation or anger, especially if other people were the subjects of my negative emotions.

Sit in a comfortable position. Begin by taking a deep breath. As you breathe out, gently close your eyes, and then continue to breathe normally. Think of yourself, focusing on your heart, not your mind, and feel the love coming from you. Begin silently with positive "May I..." statements of well-being and kindness for yourself (examples below). Once you have spent a good moment on yourself, think of a close friend or relative, and continue making silent statements, this time starting with "May you...." Spend the same amount of time on this person as you did on yourself; every person is equal and deserves equal attention, equal love. Once you have finished, progress to someone you may not know very well but do not have negative feelings toward, again spending an equal amount of time generating kind and loving "May you..." statements. Next, progress to someone who you may have difficulty loving in an active sense, spending the same amount of time on them, as well. Finally, imagine the world as a whole, with all of its people, all of its equally valuable beings, and continue making "May you..." statements. This last moment may be longer than those spent on single individuals (as this last moment includes a plethora of equal sentient creatures and not just one), or it may last the same amount of time as all of your previous moments.

Some examples of "May I/you..." statements:

- May I/you be free from harm.
- May I/you be happy.
- May I/you live with ease.
- May I/you be free from physical or mental suffering.

"Happiness is your nature. It is not wrong to desire it. What is wrong is seeking it outside when it is inside."

—Ramana Maharshi

"The idea has come to me that what I want now to do is to saturate every atom. I mean to eliminate all waste, deadness, superfluity: to give the moment whole; whatever it includes."

—Virginia Woolf

"Two thoughts cannot coexist at the same time: if the clear light of mindfulness is present, there is no room for mental twilight."

—Nyanaponika Thera

"Mindfulness is a quality that's always there. It's an illusion that there's a meditation and post-meditation period, which I always find amusing, because you're either mindful or you're not."

—Richard Gere

"The pathos of the human life teaches one that idolatry of the ego is a sham. Only by living in harmonious accord with the entire world can a person distill happiness that flows from cultivating a state of mindfulness."

—Kilroy J. Oldster

"Life is a dance. Mindfulness is witnessing that dance."

—Amit Ray

Chapter 9

Wherever You Go, There You Are: You Have All You Need

My early struggles sent me in search of something called mindfulness, even though I had no idea what I was looking for. I grew up in a family of what I describe as nutty professors—deep thinkers who liked to debate and escape into the books they read. During our family meals, everyone had a book, magazine, or newspaper in their hands. Rather than engage in conversation, my brother and parents preferred the company of literature. Even though this was many decades ago, what I saw was remarkably similar to twenty-first-century behavior, where many people engage with their digital devices at the dinner table. I recall feeling confused by this behavior. I longed for connection and presence, but I had no idea what I was looking for and I was not sure how to find it. I remember once snapping a photo of my family reading together at the dinner table. I wanted to document them all paying attention to the printed word, instead of having a lively conversation or even paying attention to the food they ate. What I experienced at home as a child was very different from what I saw around most family tables at the time.

Although I didn't know anything about mindfulness, I recognized my need for something different. It wasn't that I didn't want to read or learn. I just wanted connection, focus, and attention from my family of origin as a child, and later as a teenager. I craved presence and connection. Although I know my family members loved me, focusing on the attentional moment was not a priority, especially during mealtimes.

Later when I left home, I had my own issues with being distracted and unfocused. I was carried away by daydreams, college studies, and social life. I often lost my car keys, got into minor accidents, and a few people even speculated that I was on drugs. I was in my own inner world. My own rapid mind caused me to become discombobulated. I struggled with attention and focus. I was someone who desperately needed the tools and tricks of mindfulness to lead a happier, more productive life.

After graduating from college, I found my way to a meditation class. I took up the practice whole-heartedly. I felt more clear, stable, and focused than ever before. I discovered meditation as a way back to the present moment. Meditation eventually led me to the philosophical and physical practice of yoga, which increased my ability to be mindful, present, and focused in a hectic world. I felt happier than ever before, and able to connect and be present with family and friends, as I had always longed to be.

"Be where you are, otherwise you will miss your life."

—Buddha

"Each place is the right place—the place where I now am can be a sacred space."

—Ravi Ravindra

"The standard way of reducing stress in our culture is to put as much energy as possible into trying to arrive at a moment that matches our preferences. This ensures that we feel some level of stress until we get there (assuming we ever will), and worse, it makes the present moment into an unacceptable place to be."

—David Cain

"Surrender to what is. Let go of what was. Have faith in what will be."

—Sonia Ricotti

"Drink your tea slowly and reverently, as if it is the axis on which the world earth revolves—slowly, evenly, without rushing toward the future."

—Thích Nhất Hạnh

"If you're always racing to the next moment, what happens to the one you're in? Slow down and enjoy the moment you're in, and live your life to the fullest."

—Nanette Mathews

Learn as You Go: What's the Best Form of Meditation?

The short answer: there is none. Meditation is ultimately a tool to help you gain mindfulness in your entire life. Each person will find that a slightly different form or style of meditation helps them the best—or perhaps they will find that they like different types for different purposes. On your journey, you get to discover what works best for you.

"The mind in its natural state can be compared to the sky, covered by layers of cloud which hide its true nature."

—Kalu Rinpoche

"Like a child standing in a beautiful park with his eyes shut tight, there's no need to imagine trees, flowers, deer, birds, and sky; we merely need to open our eyes and realize what is already here, who we already are—as soon as we stop pretending we're small or unholy."

—Bo Lozoff

". . . . ."

"Expectation has brought me disappointment. Disappointment has brought me wisdom. Acceptance, gratitude, and appreciation have brought me joy and fulfilment."

—Rasheed Ogunlaru

. . . . .

"It is easy in the world to live after the world's opinion; it is easy in solitude to live after our own; but the great man is he who in the midst of the crowd keeps with perfect sweetness the independence of solitude."

—Ralph Waldo Emerson

Engage and Immerse: Anxiety and Relaxation Meditation (Five to Ten Minutes)

The anxiety and relaxation meditation is intended to calm you down when you're struggling with symptoms of stress, fear, or anxiety. I like to do it when I'm experiencing a moment of panic, worry, or pressure that I cannot seem to escape, especially if it's been preventing me from working or living mindfully that day.

Begin by sitting or lying down in a comfortable position. Take a deep breath in, and as you breathe out, slowly close your eyes. Take a few more normal breaths, focusing on the action of breathing, on how your body rises and falls with each and every breath. Now, gently shift your focus away from your breath and to the surface beneath you. Notice how solid the surface is: it's not going anywhere. It's there for you, holding you up. Breathe in, breathe out. You are fully supported at this moment. At this moment, you have nothing that you must do except breathe in and out. Think of the sky and the air, how they continue to exist around you, how they hold you up. Imagine a cool, refreshing breeze. Allow it to caress your skin, to comfort you as you breathe in, breath out. Allow it to transport you to a warm beach. The sand beneath you is soft but solid, holding you up. The water's temperature is just right. Imagine the ocean, its waves moving in with every intake of breath, and moving out as you exhale. The waves are washing over you, massaging you, smoothing the rough sand of your body. Take your time. You still have a few minutes left. The sky is still blue, the earth is still turning, everything is okay. All you have to do is breathe in, breathe out. Stay at the beach, stay in the waves, for as long as you need. When you're ready, take one last deep breath in, allow one last wave to wash over you, and as you breathe out, as the water recedes, you are now smooth. Everything is okay.

"What he's looking for, what he wants, is all around him, but he doesn't want that because it is all around him. Every step's an effort, both physically and spiritually, because he imagines his goal to be external and distant."

—Robert M. Pirsig

"To just be—to be—amidst all doings, achievings, and becomings. This is the natural state of mind, or original, most fundamental state of being. This is unadulterated Buddha-nature. This is like finding our balance."

—Lama Surya Das

"In this moment, there is plenty of time. In this moment, you are precisely as you should be. In this moment, there is infinite possibility."

—Victoria Moran

"When you bow, you should just bow; when you sit, you should just sit; when you eat, you should just eat."

—Shunryu Suzuki

"When you realize nothing is lacking, the whole world belongs to you."

—Lao Tzu

Get Out of Your Head and Back into Your Heart

Because the world we live in today is very much about getting in your head and staying there, many of us have to make a concentrated effort to become grounded and in touch with our bodies and the natural world around us. Grounding is the technique for centering you within your being, getting into your body and out of your head. Grounding is the way we reconnect and balance ourselves though the power of the element of earth. When you see someone driving past talking on their cell phone, you know that they are not grounded. For deep grounding, we recommend a creative visualization or, better yet, a group guided meditation.

Grounding Meditation: Walking the Path of Gratitude

Walking meditation is the simplest of rituals; one you can do every day of your life. As you walk, take the time to look and really see what is in your path. For example, my friend Eileen takes a bag with her and picks up every piece of garbage in her path. She does this as an act of love for the earth. During the ten years I have known her, she has practiced this ritual, she has probably turned a mountain of garbage into recycled glass, paper, and plastic. Eileen is *very* grounded. She is also a happy person who exudes and shares joy to all in her path. This is but one type of walking meditation, a very simple daily ritual that honors the earth and helps preserve life for all beings.

CHAPTER 10

RITUALS OF GRATITUDE

"Gratitude changes the pangs of memory into a tranquil joy."

—Dietrich Bonhoeffer

I once had the pleasure of attending a talk by Huston Smith, a preeminent scholar of the world's religions, who first came to the attention of the world when he brought a young Tibetan Buddhist monk—His Holiness the Dalai Lama—to America for the first time. Smith spoke about the continuing impact of religion in our world, most notably the strife in the Middle East over religious differences. He was at his most joyous when he spoke about his own spiritual practices. They were beautiful in their simplicity. Smith said that, upon rising each day, he did Hatha yoga for some minutes, followed by reading a few pages of sacred text, after which he meditated or prayed for at least five minutes. He would finish his morning ritual by doing a bit of yard work and some composting, which resulted in rich, dark soil and a beautiful garden that he greatly enjoys.

The entire audience smiled as they listened to this great and humble man describe the simple spiritual practices with which he began each day. I loved the irony that this premier academic, who has such a deep understanding of all the religious rituals throughout history, had created such an uncomplicated practice for himself. I left the talk inspired, and soon felt compelled to write a book of rituals that add meaning into our lives.

Whether people are conscious of it or not, our lives are centered upon ritual. The Wednesday night pizza and movie with the kids is a family ritual. It could be greatly enriched by adding a spiritual aspect—perhaps children could share the highlights of their week, or photos or memories could be added to a family album, to be treasured for generations to come. The Saturday night date is a romantic ritual, knitting circles are a growing trend, and doing yoga is replacing going to the gym as a spiritual and physical workout. People need ritual to inform and enrich their lives, to deal with stress, and above all, to create meaning in their lives.

The first step in this chapter is to become conscious of the power and possibility of ritual bringing us together. Daily spiritual practices and seasonal rituals create a life filled with blessings. Many of us were brought up with specific religious practices. Although I was brought up as a First Day Adventist, when I studied history, I kept discovering practices from the past that I felt were just as relevant today. One ancient ritual I discovered was bibliomancy, which is a form of divination developed when books were precious objects made of papyrus or vellum. Bibliomancy is a simple ritual that I have incorporated into my daily life for inspiration "from the gods." You simply open a book at random and let a word or phrase come to your attention. You thus become inspired by the essential meaning of the word.

Try bibliomancy with this book, and see what insights result.

The beauty of knowing history is that we can learn from the past and take the best of it to heart by applying it to our lives. Ritual is very much a part of our history and should be studied and applied to our lives today. Ritual gets us out of or heads and back into our bodies. It gets us into a place of spirit. By participating in rituals on a regular basis, you can grow in wisdom and feel an increasing sense of your aliveness.

Power Practice: Murcha—the Euphoric Breath

Pranayama is the fine art of breathing and controlling the flow of oxygen in and out of the lungs. Conscious breathing can vastly improve your health and make you more alert. *Murcha* is a yoga exercise for achieving a state of ecstasy through *pranayama*. *Murcha* in Sanskrit means "to retain," so *murcha* is the "retaining breath." *Murcha* will help you hold on to some of your natural energy that business drains away. Restore yourself through this ritual. Done properly, *murcha* will enhance your mental capacity, center you, and create a sense of euphoria.

Sit down on the floor or a mat and make yourself as comfortable as possible. Now close your eyes and calm yourself completely. Begin the process of *murcha* by taking a few mindful breaths. Breathe through your nose. Don't hold your breath; just breathe in and out in a natural manner, but remain aware of your breathing.

When you are ready, take a deeper breath through your nose and visualize the new air and oxygen traveling throughout your body, cleansing and relaxing you. Hold that deeper breath, bend your neck, and bring your chin as close to your lungs and chest as possible. Keep this position as long as you can do so comfortably. When you need to, raise your head again and slowly exhale through your nose. When your lungs are empty, repeat the murcha breath. Repeat this cycle of breathing five times only. After the fifth breath, notice how you feel, and be "in the moment." Like most breathing meditations, you will experience a subtle sort of ecstasy with raised energy and a sense of bliss.

In *pranayama,* it is important to remember not to place any stress on your body. Don't hold your breath beyond your comfort level. To do so is against the grain of the technique and teachings of *pranayama.*

With practice, you will notice you can hold your breath naturally and comfortably just a little bit longer each time. As with all things, *pranayama* yoga breathing gets better with practice. The beginning breath cleanses the pulmonary system and raises your energy level.

Grains of Nirvana: A Tibetan Buddhist Sand Mandala Ritual

Mandalas are sacred symbolic images traditionally used in Buddhism and Hinduism as aids for meditation. Mandalas have come into wider use in the West for healing, for spirituality, for art.

When His Holiness the Dalai Lama was in San Francisco, to honor his esteemed presence, the Asian Art Museum had a Tibetan cultural exhibit that was truly wonderful. One of the most moving aspects of the exhibit was the creation of an intricate, mosaic-like sand mandala by two Tibetan monks over a period of several days. Most astonishingly, at the end of the exhibit, the monks took the gorgeous, multihued masterpiece and simply threw it into the wind at Ocean Beach. We Westerners were thunderstruck. How could they possibly destroy this beautiful, spiritual art piece that took so long to create? The monks were quite jolly about it, laughing a lot and seeming quite unconcerned. They explained to the confused onlookers that "all of life is ephemeral and this act emphasizes nonattachment." While the sands are now mixed into the sands of the entire world, the wisdom associated with it has remained.

This six-step ritual taught by the Dalai Lama and his Tibetan monks has been handed down through centuries in the Himalayas. The process for making sand mandalas is a reflection of the concept of the "sacred circle." These mandalas are actually a way of "initiating" large groups of people, as the monks believe that Buddha intended enlightenment for all beings.

Preparation Rituals

Tibetan monks perform fairly intricate rituals prior to the construction of the mandala. They create sacred space with rites of purification, and bless the site where the mandala was made. Even the materials such as brushes, funnels, and sand receive blessings. Meditations upon the Buddha and other deities take place as the monks invite them to inhabit the mandala.

Mandala Designs

If you are feeling particularly ambitious, you can create the *Kalachkara Tantra,* or the "Wheel of Time," which is the sand mandala the Tibetan monks created in San Francisco. This mandala is an example of the Buddha's teachings that the Dalai Lama now shares with the Western world. However, you might not have days to devote to this ritual, and so you can design your own mandala instead. Other designs for mandalas include:

Sun

Its rays are a representation of light, energy, and life. A sun mandala will represent the positive and celebrate your life, the spark and flame of existence.

Moon

In all its phases, the moon represents feminine and emotional power. Moon mandalas are wonderful for women to create in celebration of their own femininity and of womanpower throughout time. Any goddess mandala can include the symbol of the moon.

Heart

A universal symbol of love, this sweet design would make an excellent blessing to a romantic relationship or a gift to loved ones.

Triangle

It represents the Christian Holy Trinity and Egyptian spirituality and wisdom.

Downward-Pointing Triangle

It represents the "yoni yantra" and signifies the female, the element of water, as well as the mother and the ability to create. A mandala blessing for an expectant mother should include the downward-pointing triangle. Water signs Cancer, Scorpio, and Pisces would do well to honor themselves with this design.

Double Triangle or Hexagram

In tantra, this represents all of creation, the conjunction of male and female energies. The concept of infinity is also represented by this symbol. A relationship mandala, especially in the sensual realm, will work well with double triangles. If you want to connect to the great universe, the symbol of infinity is essential. This symbol is ideal for creativity mandalas. In India, the double triangle indicates Kali in union with Shiva, and it is also the symbol for the heart chakra. If you want to create a mandala for blessing a relationship or to open your heart, the hexagram is an excellent choice. Combining the heart symbol and hexagram would be a powerful love mandala.

Pentagram

Other names for the pentagram include the Wizard's Star, the Druid's Foot, the Witch's Cross, and the Star of Bethlehem. Wiccans have claimed the pentagram as their insignia. If you want to do a mandala for healing the earth, the pentagram will accomplish this quite nicely.

Square or Quadrangle

It is the sign of the four directions, the four elements, and the four seasons. The square of the day also indicates the four significant times of day—sunrise, noonday, sunset, midnight. For the ancient Hindus, the square stood for order in the universe. You can use a square to invoke the four directions in this way, to honor the elements of air, earth, fire, and water, and to mark sacred time for prayer and meditation.

Octagon or Double Square

With its eight points, this is another symbol for divine order and unification. It is a good symbol for peace on earth. Essentially an eight-pointed star, the octagon is a symbol for rebirth and renewal, and for the wheel of the year. The octagon is believed to have magical powers, as does the pentacle or pentagram, when drawn in one line. In this case, they are believed to indicate sacred space. An octagon is a very good symbol to include in a mandala when you are embarking on a new phase of your life—a new home, job, relationship, a "new you"—that can be blessed in this manner.

Knotwork and the "Knot of Eternity"

These are lovely symbols of unity. In Buddhist tradition, knotwork represents contemplation and meditation. Celtic knotwork symbolizes the eternal flow of energy and life.

Lotus

This flower represents beauty, creation, renewal, and in Buddhism, the search for enlightenment. If the lotus has twelve petals, it represents the energy of the sun. If it has sixteen petals, it is the symbol for the moon. The most spiritual mandalas will likely contain the image of the lotus.

If you don't have access to a Tibetan temple space, you can create a sacred temple space in your own home. Ideally, your windows allow sacred light to fall upon the design. This is an artistic endeavor; you are making sacred art. If you do your best work at night, be sure to have adequate lighting. It is also a good idea to reduce the possibilities of distractions and interruptions. It is strongly suggested to turn off phones and television, to create as peaceful an environment as possible.

Bless the space in a fashion of your own choosing. Tibetan monks always use Tibetan incense and have images of Buddha to venerate his memory and teachings.

Clarify Your Intention

Why do you want to create a sand mandala? Your reason is your intention, and is the focus of your ritual. One basic guideline is that the creation of a sand mandala should be "for the greater good." Some examples of reasons to create a specific sand mandala include:

- To help create world peace
- To bring renewed health to body and spirit
- To bless a new home
- To bless and bring joy to all people in your life

Blessing the Supplies

Call upon the Buddha and beloved ancestors who have passed on to bless your materials. In this case, you have multiple packets of colored sand, readily available at any craft store, which you need to imbue with the energy of the divine. Simply place the packets on the surface of the mandala design you have chosen.

Hold your hand over the sand and the mandala design you have drawn and visualize the light of the universe and of the sun pouring through you and through your hands to the sand and the design. If you feel a personal connection to any benevolent spirits such as angels, the Buddha, or gods or goddesses, you should call upon them to also bless your efforts and the material with their sacred energy.

You may notice a warming of your hands as you continue concentrating "in the light." Invoke aloud or pray silently to your benevolent guardians to bless your endeavor.

Meditation

Tibetan monks also suggest doing a meditative movement, such as tai chi or yoga, to stretch and relax both body and mind prior to entering the intense mental stillness and physicality demanded by the construction of the sand mandala. Essentially, you are bent over for quite a long time in deep concentration, and you need to prepare yourself physically and mentally for this direction of your energies. Movement is a way of centering yourself.

In addition to the movement, you should also meditate and surround yourself with the energy of light and love. Sit on the floor, lotus fashion, and in a whispered chant, repeat the Sanskrit word *Om* over and over again. Manage your breathing, slowly and deeply. You will soon feel your heart and mind surrounded by energy. Now, focus on your intention again, and ponder any new clarity of thought.

Painting with Sand

With your intention set clearly in your mind and being, pour sand into a funnel (or a small bag with a tiny hole in the bottom), and let it fall gently upon the design you have drawn, one color at a time, allowing the divine to guide you. If you are creating a specific image, you can copy its color and design; otherwise, allow creation and inspiration to flow through you. Creating the design slowly and carefully is key, but in case of accident, a damp sponge applied with care will remove any random sand. It is important to remember that there are no "mistakes" in this art; you are in the safety of the sacred space you create with the help of the celestial.

When you have finished your sand mandala, you will see it and feel it and know it in your heart. However, physical completion of the sand mandala is not the end.

Dismantling Your Mandala

While dismantling the sand mandala is counterintuitive to the Western mind, it is actually the next step in the ritual. When you are ready, take some time to look at your mandala and contemplate the image you have created. Look deeply and quietly and "receive" any insights or messages during meditation.

Offer thanks to the divine beings who helped you in this ritual and who help you in your daily life. Now take a small brush and move the sand to the center of the mandala.

Scattering the Sand

When I learned the art of creating a sand mandala, the monks who taught me carried their sand to the Pacific Ocean. It is in accordance with the Tibetan tradition that the scattering take place at the nearest body of water, accompanied by chanting and song. If you have no water nearby, but there is a garden or park near your home, you might feel like performing the scattering aspect of the ritual there to keep the blessing energy nearby.

Close the ritual by dedicating the blessing energy of the mandala to the greater good of the universe.

First	root (base of spine)	**red**	security, survival
Second	sacral	**orange**	pleasure
Third	solar plexus	**yellow**	divine, personal power
Fourth	heart	**green**	abundance, love, serenity
Fifth	throat	**blue**	creativity, originality
Sixth	third eye	**indigo**	intuitiveness, perception
Seventh	crown	**violet**	holy bliss, all is one

Color Connection

Color is a form of energy that can be broken down by individual vibrations. We use colors in our homes and at work to affect moods. The right colors can calm, energize, or even romanticize a setting. Colors promote many desired states of being. Anyone using color is tuning in to the vibration frequency of that particular color. Some psychics have the skills and training to read your aura; they can literally see the energy radiating out from your body.

Other colors not in the spectrum or chakra exist in crystals and stones, and are significant in their own right: brown, gray, black, white, silver, and gold.

- **Brown:** The color of humility and poverty. Represents safety and the home.

- **Gray:** The color of grief and mourning. Symbolized resurrection in medieval times. Gray is the first color the human eye can perceive in infancy.

- **Black:** Protection and strength. Fortifies your personal energies and gives them more inner authority. In Africa, symbolizes fertile, life-giving, rich earth, and nourishing rain.

- **White:** Purity, peace, patience, and protection. Some cultures associate white with death.

- **Silver:** Relates to communication and greater access to the universe. Indicates a lunar connection or female energy.

- **Gold:** Direct connection to God. Facilitates wealth and ease.

POWER THOUGHTS: YOUR CONTEMPLATION STATION

. . . .

"People get into a heavy-duty sin and guilt trip, feeling that if things are going wrong, that means that they did something bad and they are being punished. That's not the idea at all. The idea of karma is that you continually get the teachings that you need to open your heart. To the degree that you didn't understand in the past how to stop protecting your soft spot, how to stop armoring your heart, you're given this gift of teachings in the form of your life, to give you everything you need to open further."

—Pema Chödrön

"Mindfulness is a way of befriending ourselves and our experience."

—Jon Kabat-Zinn

"The most precious gift we can offer others is our presence. When mindfulness embraces those we love, they will bloom like flowers."

—Thích Nhất Hạnh

"If the doors of perception were cleansed, everything would appear to man as it is, infinite."

—William Blake

Balinese Full Moon Ceremony

Nearly every temple and Bali celebrates this monthly event. Essential elements for this ritual are incense, offerings of fruit and lots of flowers, rice, and holy or blessed water.

Gather a group of like-minded folks and head to the nearest body of water—a lake, pond, creek, river, or the ocean. Nature will be your temple. Begin by sitting in a circle and making garlands of flowers. You should talk, laugh, or be silent as you wish, but most important, be comfortable. When everyone is settled with a garland of flowers, place the garland around the neck of another person. Light the incense and set the rice and holy water in the middle of the circle.

Go around the circle and offer the water to people, sprinkling it on them gently with your fingertips in the Balinese fashion, and offer everyone a cupful of the holy water to rinse their mouths with so the worst they speak will be holier. Each person should make a fruit or flower offering to the gods, and lay it near the cleansing smoke of incense. After the offerings are made, everyone should anoint their neighbor's forehead with grains of rice and speak blessings aloud for each person. If a body of water is accessible, get wet, even if it is just to dip your hands or walk in the water.

Silently acknowledge the blessings in your life through prayer and meditation, and again, give quiet thanks to the gods for the gift of your life. Unlike most Western-based rituals, there is not much talking during the Balinese Full Moon Ritual. Bask in the tranquility and listen to your thoughts.

Pung-Mul Nori

Pung-Mul Nori is a full moon ritual that has been performed for about two thousand years and continues to this day. Korean traditional folklore combines ritual, acrobatics, dance, and music. *Toyo Ongaku*, the music for this ritual, has remained popular since ancient times, when it was performed day and night to protect crops and dispel evil spirits.

Developed by and for Korean farmers, this ritual was devised to help them keep up their strength and their spirits during the exhausting labor of the planting and harvesting seasons. Many years ago, it was especially important for everyone in the community to participate in this expression of thanksgiving. Every man, woman, and child who was physically able to do so had to sing, dance, drum, play instruments, and perform acrobatics. The word *Nori* in Pung-Mul Nori means "to play," and indeed, this is one of the most playful of all the world's moon rituals.

Walking the Labyrinth: A Path of Grace to the Inner Self

At the Grace Cathedral on California Street in San Francisco, scholar Lauren Artress oversaw the installation of not one but two labyrinths. Sue Patton Thoele, author of *The Woman's Book of Soul,* invited me to go there one fine day a few years ago. I remember squeezing it into my schedule, feeling hurried, and hoping it would not take more than half an hour or so. I am a bit embarrassed to admit this, but I know I am not the only busy life-juggler who has found herself surprised by the sacred.

When we got there, a magnificent stillness presided over the entire cathedral. We chose the indoor labyrinth instead of the outdoor one, as there was a distinct chill in the foggy air that day. We read the simple instructions and, as told, removed our shoes to tread the path in bare or stocking feet. For my part, I had already begun to calm down, thanks to the peaceful atmosphere. As I walked in the light of the stained glass shadows, my schedule started to seem petty. Suddenly it seemed as if I could give this just a little more time.

Sue, an experienced labyrinth walker, had gone ahead and seemed to be in a reverie, as did the tourists, students, and random folks who populated the nave. I checked the instructions again just to make sure I performed my barefoot ritual "correctly."

As I began, thoughts skittered through my head, and I had to struggle to focus and be in the now. With no small amount of effort, I was able to have an authentic experience. As I walked the winding path, a replica of the labyrinth on the floor of Chartres Cathedral, I felt a growing excitement. This was meaningful; perhaps there was hope even for me and my over-busy "monkey mind." My breathing relaxed, and I had a growing sense that I was going somewhere. When I reached the center of the labyrinth, I looked up at the soaring high ceiling of Grace Cathedral. At that exact moment, the sun struck a stained glass window and a golden shaft of light shone directly upon me. I was mystified, and a beaming Sue, having completed her walk, noticed what was happening to me. I studied the window to see if there was any kind of symbol from which to draw further meaning. To my astonishment, the sun had lit up a window that contained the medieval tableau of a sword in a rock. As a lapsed medieval scholar, I immediately recognized Excalibur of the famous Arthurian legend. Tears came into my eyes, and I realized this was a message. I had often felt a bit guilty for not completing my master's degree in medieval studies. At that moment, I knew I had to complete that quest. One of my specializations was the Arthurian saga, and here, in no uncertain terms, Arthur's sword had spoken to me as I stood in the center of the labyrinth. Exhilarated, I retraced my steps, and returned to where I entered, brimming with joy.

Now, I truly understand what it means to be "illuminated."

Walking Meditation: How to Walk the Labyrinth

The labyrinth represented wholeness to the ancients, combining the circle and the spiral in one archetypal image. The labyrinth is unicursal, meaning there is only one path, both in and out. Put simply, it is a journey into the self, into your own center, and back into the world again. As a prayer and meditation tool, labyrinths are peerless; they awaken intuition.

Do your best to relax before you enter. Deep breaths will help a great deal. If you have a specific question in mind, think it or whisper it to yourself. You will meet others on the pilgrim's path as you are walking; simply step aside and let them continue on their journey as you do the same. The three stages of the labyrinth walk are as follows:

Purgation: Here is where you free your mind of all worldly concerns. It is a release, a letting go. Still your mind and open your heart. Shed worries and emotion as you step out on the path.

Illumination: When you have come to the center, you are in the place of illumination. Here, you should stay as long as you feel the need to pray and meditate. In this quiet center, the heart of the labyrinth, you will receive messages from the divine or from your own higher power. Illumination can also come from deep inside yourself.

Union: This last phase is where you will experience union with the divine. Lauren Artress says that as you "walk the labyrinth you become more empowered to find and do the work you feel your soul requires."

Use the rituals in this chapter to become one with yourself and find peace within. May you use this learned tranquility to better participate in other rituals that focus on important aspects of your life.

The Sukhavti: Buddhist Ritual for Death

A few years ago, I attended a memorial service for my dear friend Duncan's mother, Maggie. Maggie was an amazing woman. Born into a middle-class Jewish family, she thrived in the hippie years, traveling the world and experimenting with many different religions. Eventually the road took her to Buddhist shrines and ashrams, places of study and meditation. Maggie attended the esteemed Naropa Institute in Boulder, Colorado, and delved deeply into her practice, meditating for hours on end. While in an ashram in Nova Scotia, keeping a vow of silence, she became very ill and died. The occasion of her death was observed by the Buddhist ritual, *Sukhavti*.

Courtesy of the late Maggie's son, Duncan McCloud, here is a portion of the prayer from the funeral ritual. It is taken from sacred Tibetan texts and was translated by Maggie herself.

Prayer for Reincarnation

Whose outstanding deeds give endless
glory to beings
Whose mere remembrance banishes Death
With love, we speak this prayer for
reincarnation and rebirth
May I be free of sadness and misery
May I still feel the love of those I have left behind
May I pass by the demons
May I remember well my faith and consolation
May I see for myself Amitabha, the Greatest
Teacher of us all,
Supreme Being Highest and Lord of All
May I see the greatness and the glory.
At the moment of my death, may I
receive enlightenment
May I be reborn.

The *Sukhavti* is a series of little vignettes, stories, and collected memories of the dead. The Buddhists believe in reincarnation, that death is a step in the soul's continuing journey. The purpose of the *Sukhavti* is to help talk the newly dead spirit through the *bardos*, which are a sort of continuum through which the spirit must pass. Safe passage is not guaranteed, for the deceased must get past Tibetan demons of terrible aspect.

At Maggie's service, to help her through the *bardos*, people said sweet things, sad things, funny things, and extremely honest things about her. In fact, it is of the utmost importance to be very frank and tell the truth, as the honesty will help the spirit through the *bardos*.

Steps for a Successful Sukhavti

1. Gather Tibetan temple incense and flowers, and invite people to a room set up for meditation with floor mats and pillows. If possible, invite the recently passed person's spiritual teacher or someone well acquainted with both Tibetan Buddhism and the subject of the service.

2. Begin with a statement of the purpose of the *Sukhavti* for those who have never attended one, followed by a ten-minute silent meditation.

3. Light incense and place it together with flowers in front of a photo or image of the recently passed person.

4. Invite anyone who has anything to say about the person to speak, explaining the helpfulness of truth and honesty in aiding the spirit through the *bardos*. The serene nature of this Buddhist ceremony allows for silence and reflection; speaking should not be forced.

Again, although this method of honoring the dead was unusual to my Western mind, Maggie's ritual was one of the most meaningful ceremonies I have ever experienced.

In this look at life's passages, we have made the journey from birth to death and many phases in between. The more rituals you create and perform to acknowledge these phases of human life, the richer your life will be.

Invoking the Blessing of Nikadama

In China and Tibet, mountains hold a special place in mythology and religion because they are so close to the sky. Tibetan Buddhists bring down the blessings of one of their most benevolent deities, Nikadama, the female protection deity, who lives high in the Himalaya Mountains. To get her attention, tie strings of Tibetan prayer flags or white silk scarves to the trees and bushes near your home or in your yard. If you live in the city, you can hang them at your door to fly in the breeze. Every time the flags and offering scarves flutter in the wind, Nikadama is blessing you! Here is a very simple ritual you can perform alone or with loved ones to bring luck and blessings during the waxing moon. Spring is the best time to do this, but any waxing moon will bring fortune and providence.

⟩ Tibetan Prayer Flag 101

The color symbology of a string of Tibetan prayer flags comes from hundreds of years of tradition. Monks always fly the blue flag highest and it should be at the top of the string of flags, as it symbolizes the closest you can get to higher consciousness. Other colors that represent aspects of nature are as follows:

Blue: Sky

White: Cloud

Red: Fire

Green: Water

Yellow: Earth

Centering: Getting Grounded in Yourself

The best way to prepare for personal ritual is to center yourself. I call this "doing a readjustment," and I believe this is especially important in our overscheduled and busy world. Doing a readjustment helps pull you back into yourself, and gets your priorities back on track. Only when you are truly centered can you do the true inner work of self-development that is at the core of ritual.

Centering takes many forms. Experiment on your own to find out what works best for you. My friend Kat Sanborn, for example, does a quick meditation that she calls "the chakra check-in." The chakra system comprises energy points in the astral body, and is also associated with various endocrine glands in the physical body. My friend closes her eyes and sits lotus fashion (if possible, but if you are on a bus or in a meeting you can do this centering exercise just sitting down, feet on the floor), and visualizes the light and color of each chakra. She visualizes each chakra and mentally runs energy up and down her spine, from bottom to top, pausing at each chakra point. After she does this a few times, a soothing calm surrounds her. I have seen her perform her "chakra check-in" at trade shows and in hotel lobbies, surrounded by the hubbub of many people. She is an ocean of calm at the center of a storm. By working with your chakras, you can become much more in touch with your body and soul.

The root chakra is at the base of your spine and is associated with passion, survival, and security and the color red. Above it is the sacral chakra in the abdominal region, which corresponds to such physical urges as hunger and sex, and its color is orange. The solar plexus chakra is yellow, and is associated with personal power. The throat chakra is blue, and is considered the center of communication. The third eye chakra is located in the center of your forehead, and is associated with intuition and the color indigo. The crown chakra, at the very top of your head, is your connection to the universe, and it is violet in color.

Prior to performing a ritual, try this centering exercise. Take a comfortable sitting position and find your pulse. Keep your fingers on your pulse until you feel the steady rhythm of your own heart.

Now begin slowly breathing in rhythm with your heartbeat. Inhale for four beats, hold for four beats, and then exhale for five beats. Repeat this pattern for six cycles. People have reported that although it seems hard to match up with the heartbeat at first, with a little bit of practice, your breath and heartbeat will synchronize. Your entire body will relax and all physical functions will seem slower and more natural than ever before.

Candle Centering

Another excellent way to center yourself is to light a candle and meditate on it. By focusing on the flame, you bring your being and awareness into focus. You can take candle centering a step further with this spell for new insight into your life.

1. Place one candle on your altar or "centering station." Light your favorite meditation incense. For me, *nag champa* immediately sanctifies any space and creates a sacred aura.

2. Scratch your name into the candle with the tip of your knife. Next, scratch your hope into the candle.

3. Light your candle and recite:
   This candle burns for me
   Here burns my hope for...
   Here burns the flame of insight
   May I see clearly in this new light

4. Sit with your eyes closed for a few minutes and picture yourself enacting your hopes and desires. You are setting your intention. Picture yourself in the company of people who inspire and teach you, those who bring insight and new light into your life. Let the candle burn down completely.

"We speculate, dream, strategize, and plan for these 'conditions of happiness' we want to have in the future, and we continually chase after that future, even while we sleep. We may have fears about the future because we don't know how it's going to turn out, and these worries and anxieties keep us from enjoying being here now."

—Thích Nhất Hạnh

"Perfection of character is this: to live each day as if it were your last, without frenzy, without apathy, without pretense."

—Marcus Aurelius

"Throughout this life, you can never be certain of living long enough to take another breath."

—Huang Po

> *"It's only when we truly know and understand that we have a limited time on earth—and that we have no way of knowing when our time is up—that we will begin to live each day to the fullest, as if it was the only one we had."*

—Elisabeth Kübler-Ross

> *"Do every act of your life as though it were the very last act of your life."*

—Marcus Aurelius

> *"Most people treat the present moment as if it were an obstacle that they need to overcome. Since the present moment is life itself, it is an insane way to live."*

—Eckhart Tolle

A Compassionate Heart

The human body is made mostly of water, and our connection to this sacred element is part of our very being. People are especially drawn to the ocean, whose water is a blend of minerals and water similar to the chemical mix of our blood. Have you ever noticed how blissful you can feel when you're at the beach? The negative ions produced by water are soothing and create an overwhelming sense of optimism. In the presence of water, we feel refreshed. The ocean tides are a rhythm of life and a regulating force of nature.

Water cleanses and restores us, determines our climate, enriches our crops and forests. Water has long been used in ritual and continues to this day to be employed by nearly every culture. In India, the sacred Ganges River cleanses the souls of Hindus from birth through death, when they often float off to eternity in a river burial. Christian baptisms are done with the sacrament of water. The Chinese deity Kuan Yin, goddess of compassion, offers spiritual seekers the comfort and solace of a holy lake. Aphrodite herself rose up from the ocean, and the Yoruban divinity, Ymoja (Yemaya in Brazil and Cuba), is believed to rule all the waters of the earth.

I was born with both my natal sun and moon in the astrological sign of Pisces. As a double Pisces, I receive much spiritual substance from water and turn to my element for succor. Water is the element that rules Pisces, Cancer, and Scorpio. It reconnects water folk with their native element, and keeps them in tune with their true nature.

The Japanese have elevated water ritual to the level of an art form with baths, water meditations, water gardens, and tea ceremonies. Through the centuries, they have perfected the presentation of tea as an inventive and spiritual practice.

The following rituals concentrate on this life-sustaining and significant element.

Taking the Waters—a Releasing Ritual

Sarasvati is a Hindu goddess of the arts, and originally a river goddess. She is invoked by individuals seeking to improve the flow of their creativity and self-transformation.

A bath blessing that will both relax and purify you is a rare and wonderful thing. To prepare yourself, place one quart of rough sea or Epsom salts in a large bowl. Add the juice from six freshly squeezed lemons, half a cup of sesame oil, and a few drops of rose and jasmine oils. Stir until the mixture is completely moistened. You can add more sesame oil if necessary, but do not add more lemon because it will make the mixture overly astringent and potentially irritating to your skin.

When your tub is one-third full, add one-quarter of the salt mixture under the faucet. Breathe in deeply ten times, inhaling and exhaling fully before you do this recitation. You may start to feel a tingling at the crown of your head. The water should still be running when you proclaim:

> Sarasvati, O Harmonious One,
> Goddess and mistress, I ask your guidance.
> Remove from me any impurities
> of heart, spirit, and mind, I open myself to you.
> My wish is to once again become whole,
> free of pain, sadness, and all that is better in me.

When the tub is full, it is time to step inside and breathe deeply ten more times. Repeat the prayer to Sarasvati, and use the rest of the salt to gently massage your body. Rest and rejuvenate as long as you like, allowing yourself to feel refreshed and renewed by the ministrations of this Hindu goddess of harmony and artistry, from whom eloquence, inspiration, and blessings flow.

Designing Your Own Water Rituals

From the depths of your imagination, you can create a water ritual of your own by invoking other water deities. By inviting the energy of water into your sacred space, you will find the words will flow into you as you fashion ceremonial language appropriate to that god or goddess.

You can create your own ceremonies and spells to call forth the power of water for psychic development such as dream work, emotional balance, healing, creativity, joy, love, and letting go.

Heart-Opening Yoga

The elephant-headed Ganesha is the Indian god who helps overcome all obstacles. What better way to start the New Year than with this mighty deity at your side? Ganesha is beloved in India, where he is also called *Vighnaharta*, the "Lord and Destroyer of Obstacles." When people seek success in work or school, they turn to this jolly elephant god. I keep a little bronze statue of a supine Ganesha on my computer.

Mudra is a type of yoga you do with your hands. It is also called "finger power points." This is a portable yoga that you can do anywhere—on the bus, in your car, at your desk, even walking down the street. This is a marvelous way to calm yourself and handle stress. Buddha statues are usually shown with the hands in a *mudra*.

The very easy *Ganesha mudra* begins by holding your left hand in front of your chest with the palm facing outward, away from your body. Bend your fingers. Grasp your left fingers with your right finders bent, toward your body.

Move the hands to the level of your heart, right in front of your chest. Exhale vigorously and gently try to pull your hands apart without releasing the grip. This will create tensions in your upper arms and chest area, exercising those muscles.

Now relax those muscles while inhaling. Repeat these steps six times, then place both your hands on your sternum in the Ganesha clasping position. Note the energy and heat you feel in your body. Now repeat six times with your hands facing in the reversed positions.

The *Ganesha mudra* opens the fourth chakra and gives us "heart"—courage, confidence, and good feelings toward others. It opens us up to new encounters and new, positive experiences. Performed once a day, this is a marvelous way to strengthen your upper body. It is also believed to open the bronchial tubes and stimulate that area.

BE GRATEFUL FOR EACH OTHER, BE GRATEFUL TOGETHER

In closing, we thought we would share with you one last way that you can express all of this newfound gratitude, and that is by opening a "Gratitude Circle." The idea is simple. A Gratitude Circle is a place for sharing stories, photos, prayers of gratitude, and videos with friends and loved ones. The more people you can get to align with you, the sooner you will discover the positive power of gratitude and reap the many benefits that come from doing so. Now, we want to spread that gift and help you become cheerleaders for others who have tapped into the power of thankfulness, by forming your own Gratitude Circle.

By creating a Gratitude Circle, you can join us in being grateful. Connect with others in this special group that's dedicated to honoring the simple phrases, "Thank you," and "I am grateful for...." We know firsthand that once you start a thankfulness circle, it won't take long for others to join in, and the combined power of your gratitude will permeate and bless your everyday being.

There are several ways you can create a Gratitude Circle or Group. I'll make it easy for you with some tips.

Opening to Thankfulness

1. As the organizer of the Gratitude Circle, consider yourself the host or hostess, almost as if you have invited a group of friends—or people you hope to become friends—to your dinner table. Your role is to help guide conversations and serve up a feast (of interesting stories about gratitude or nuggets of information to share) that will keep the conversations meaningful, inspiring, and ultimately bring to life the power of gratitude in all the lives of those who have gathered.

2. Create a mission or set of goals for your Gratitude Circle. Create a plan for guiding your group through the practice of gratitude. What do you want to accomplish? How will you manifest gratitude in your own life and the lives of those in your circle? Will you share stories, inspiring quotes, guided meditations?

3. Decide whether to meet online or in-person. The exciting thing about the internet, is that you can create a Gratitude Circle and community online, and connect friends and colleagues from across the country—and the world. Or you may prefer to create an in-person circle with friends in your neighborhood or town.

4. Send out invites, Evites, and make phone calls to invite members to your Gratitude Circle. Ask everyone to invite a friend and spread the word about your new group.

5.   Select a meet-up place. Often, organizers will invite people to meet at their own home. Or you may opt for a local coffee shop or other comfortable meeting place where you can gather regularly.

6.   Create a calendar of meet-up dates, and distribute to your group.

7.   Create Gratitude Circle materials. In this book, we have lots of prompts for discussions about gratitude and thankfulness. Please feel free to tap into these resources.

8.   Spread the good news about what being thankful can accomplish, as it manifests in your life and the lives of your friends, family, and members of your Gratitude Circle.

Circles of Grace

Those simple suggestions should help you and your Gratitude Circle get started. Remember, nothing is cast in stone, and you can feel free to improvise until you find your comfort zone. We guarantee you will come away from these gatherings feeling inspired, challenged, and with exciting new ideas to share.

First, begin by welcoming your guests. Go around the circle, with each person introducing themself. For example, "I am Mary Smith, and I live in Ohio. I am a writer, literacy volunteer, and mother of two." Next, read a passage of poetry, prayer, or prose. We recommend sections from either the introduction or the beginning of chapter two of this book. Now, go clockwise around the circle, and ask each participant why she or he is here, and what spiritual sustenance he or she is seeking.

Ask a volunteer to read her favorite prayer or quote about being thankful. These group gatherings are wonderful, but personal sharing and goal discussion can be intimidating at first, so be mindful of your group, and you'll sense when you will need to wrap things up. Always end on a high note by asking each person to share gratitude. May your transformation be your inspiration!

The Five Remembrances of Buddha

I am of the nature to grow old.
There is no way to escape growing old.
I am of the nature to have ill-health.
There is no way to escape having ill-health.
I am of the nature to die.
There is no way to escape death.
All that is dear to me and everyone I love
are of the nature to change.
There is no way to escape being separated from them.
My actions are my only true belongings.
I cannot escape the consequences of my actions.
My actions are the ground on which I stand.

—Buddha

About the Author

Becca Anderson comes from a long line of preachers and teachers from Ohio and Kentucky. The teacher side of her family led her to become a women's studies scholar and the author of *The Book of Awesome Women* and several other works. An avid collector of meditations, prayers, and blessings, she helps run a "Gratitude and Grace Circle" that meets monthly at homes, churches, and bookstores in the San Francisco Bay Area, where she currently resides. Becca Anderson credits her spiritual practice with helping her recover from cancer and wants to share this with anyone who is facing difficulty in their life.

Author of *Think Happy to Stay Happy* and *Every Day Thankful,* Becca Anderson shares her inspirational writings and suggested acts of kindness at TheDailyInspoBlog. wordpress.com.

Mango Publishing, established in 2014, publishes an eclectic list of books by diverse authors—both new and established voices—on topics ranging from business, personal growth, women's empowerment, LGBTQ studies, health, and spirituality to history, popular culture, time management, decluttering, lifestyle, mental wellness, aging, and sustainable living. We were recently named 2019's #1 fastest growing independent publisher by Publishers Weekly. Our success is driven by our main goal, which is to publish high quality books that will entertain readers as well as make a positive difference in their lives.

Our readers are our most important resource; we value your input, suggestions, and ideas. We'd love to hear from you—after all, we are publishing books for you!

Please stay in touch with us and follow us at:

Facebook: Mango Publishing
Twitter: @MangoPublishing
Instagram: @MangoPublishing
LinkedIn: Mango Publishing
Pinterest: Mango Publishing

Sign up for our newsletter at www.mango.bz and receive a free book!

Join us on Mango's journey to reinvent publishing, one book at a time.